Access 97 for Windows Made Simple

Moira Stephen

Routledge
Taylor & Francis Group

LONDON AND NEW YORK

First published 1997 by Made Simple

2 Park Square, Milton Park, Abingdon, Oxon OX14 4RN
711 Third Avenue, New York, NY 10017, USA

Routledge is an imprint of the Taylor & Francis Group, an informa business

First issued in hardback 2017

British Library Cataloguing in Publication Data
A catalogue record for this book is available from the British Library

ISBN 978-0-7506-3800-5 (pbk)
ISBN 978-1-138-43621-3 (hbk)

Typeset by P.K.McBride, Southampton

Archtype, Bash Casual, Cotswold and Gravity fonts from Advanced Graphics Ltd
Icons designed by Sarah Ward © 1994
Transferred to digital printing 2006

Contents

Preface

The computer is about as simple as a spacecraft, and who ever let an untrained spaceman loose? You pick up a manual that weighs more than your birth-weight, open it and find that its written in computerspeak. You see messages on the screen that look like code and the thing even makes noises. No wonder that you feel it's your lucky day if everything goes right. What do you do if everything goes wrong? Give up.

Training helps. Being able to type helps. Experience helps. This book helps, by providing training and assisting with experience. It can't help you if you always manage to hit the wrong keys, but it can tell you which are the right ones and what to do when you hit the wrong ones. After some time, even the dreaded manual will start to make sense, just because you know what the writers are wittering on about.

Computing is not black magic. You don't need luck or charms, just a bit of understanding. The problem is that the programs that are used nowadays look simple but aren't. Most of them are crammed with features you don't need – but how do you know what you don't need? This book shows you what is essential and guides you through it. You will know how to make an action work and why. The less essential bits can wait – and once you start to use a program with confidence you can tackle these bits for yourself.

The writers of this series have all been through it. We know your time is valuable, and you don't want to waste it. You don't buy books on computer subjects to read jokes or be told that you are a dummy. You want to find what you need and be shown how to achieve it. Here, at last, you can.

1 Getting Started

What is a database?

A **database** is simply a collection of data. For example, it may be an address list, employee details or details about items in stock.

Access is a **relational** database – this means that all related data is stored in one place. If you are storing data about your business, you could have your employee data, customer data, product data, supplier data, etc. all stored in your company database.

Table

In a relational database, all the data on one topic is stored in a **table**. You would have a table for your employee data, a table for your customer data, a table for your product data, etc. If your database requirements are fairly simple, you might have only one table in your database. If your requirements are more complex, your database may contain several tables.

The data in the table is structured in a way that will allow you to interrogate the data when and as required. All of the data on one item, e.g. an employee or a stock item, is held in the **record** for that employee or stock item, within the appropriate table.

Record

A **record** contains information about a single item in your table. All the detail relating to one employee will be held in that employee's record. All the detail on a customer will be held in a record for that customer. The information is broken down into several **fields**.

Tip

If you've never used a database package before, I suggest you read through the next few pages carefully. Database concepts and jargon are not difficult, but you need to appreciate how a database works (in theory) and to become familiar with some of the jargon you will come across. If you're already familiar with databases you can move on to 'Getting into Access' (page 8).

Field

A **field** is a piece of data within a record. In an employee's record things like forename, surname, job title, address, age, salary, etc. would all be held in separate fields. In a stock item record, you would have fields for stock number, description, price, etc.

Each field has a name that identifies it.

Company database file

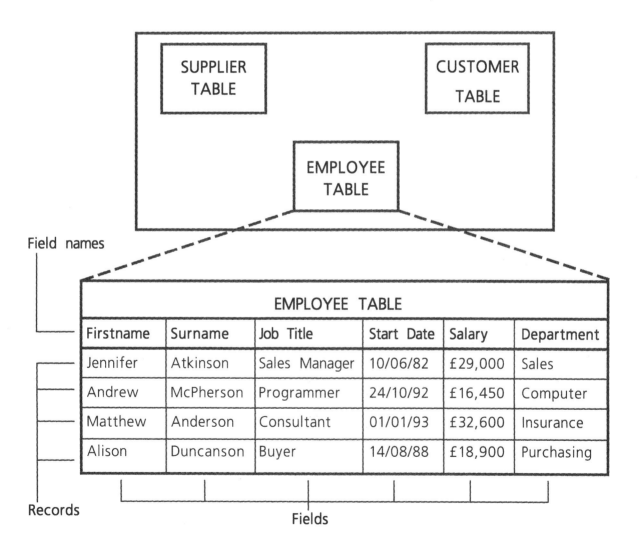

Field names

Records

Fields

Access objects

When working in Access, you find six different types of **objects** that are used to input, display, interrogate, print and automate your work. These objects are listed on the tabs in the Database window.

Tables

Tables are the most important object in your database. Tables are used for data entry, viewing data and displaying the results of queries (see Chapters 3-9).

In a table, each record is displayed as a row and each field is displayed as a column. You can display a number of records on the screen at any one time, and as many fields as will fit on your screen. Any records or fields not displayed can be scrolled into view as required.

Queries

You use **queries** to locate specific records within your tables. You might want to extract records that meet specific selection criteria (e.g. all employees on Grade G in the accounts department). When you run a query, the results are displayed in a table (see Chapter 9).

Forms

You can use **forms** to provide an alternative to tables for data entry and viewing records. With forms, you arrange the fields as required on the screen – you can design your forms to look like the printed forms (invoices, order forms, etc.) that you use.

When you use forms, you display one record at a time on your screen (see Chapter 10).

Reports

Reports can be used to produce various printed outputs from data in your database. Using reports, the same database can produce a list of customers in a certain area, a set of mailing labels for your letters, or a report on how much each customer owes you, (see Chapter 11).

Macros **and Modules**

Macros and **modules** are used to automate the way you use Access, and can be used to build some very sophisticated applications.

They are well beyond the scope of a Made Simple book!

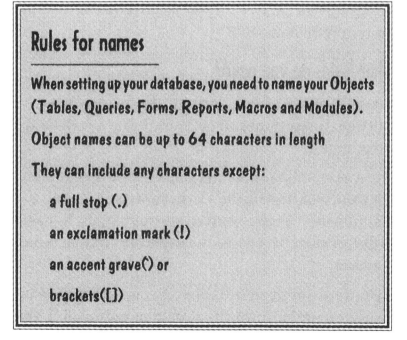

Rules for names

When setting up your database, you need to name your Objects (Tables, Queries, Forms, Reports, Macros and Modules).

Object names can be up to 64 characters in length

They can include any characters except:

    a full stop (.)

    an exclamation mark (!)

    an accent grave(`) or

    brackets([])

Tip

Learn to recognise these tabs — they can speed up your work.

Preparing your data

The most important (and often difficult) stage in setting up your database takes place away from the computer. Before you set up a database you must get your data organised.

You must ask yourself two key questions:

- What do I want to store?
- What information do I want to get out of my database?

NB   You must also work out your answers to these two questions!!

Once you've decided what you are storing and what use you intend to make of the data, you are ready to start designing your database. Again, much of this can be done away from the computer.

What fields do you need?

You must break the data down into the smallest units you will want to search or sort on. Each of these must be in a separate field.

If you were setting up names, you would probably break the name into three fields – Title, Firstname (or Initials) and Surname. This way you can sort the file into Surname order, or search for someone using the Firstname and Surname.

If you were storing addresses, you would probably want separate fields for Town/city, Region and/or Country. You can then sort your records into order on any of these fields, or locate records by specifying appropriate search criteria. For example, using Town/city and Country fields, you could search for addresses in Perth (Town/city),

Tip

When planning your database, take a small sample of the data to be stored and examine it carefully. Break the detail on each item into small units for sorting and searching. You can then start to work out what fields will be needed to enable you to store all the necessary data for each item.

Australia (Country) rather than Perth (Town/city), Scotland (Country).

How big are the fields?

You must also decide how much space is required for each field. The space you allocate must be long enough to accommodate the longest item that might go there. How long is the longest surname you want to store? If in doubt, take a sample of some typical names (McDonald, Peterson, MacKenzie, Harvey-Jones?) and add a few more characters to the longest one to be sure. An error in field size isn't as serious as an error in record structure as field sizes can be expanded without existing data being affected.

It is very important that you spend time organising and structuring your data before you start to computerise it - it'll save you a lot of time and frustration in the long run!

Take note

You can specify the size of text and number fields.

Text fields can be up to 255 characters in length (the default is 50).

Number field sizes have several options (see Field Size in the on-line Help).

Take note

Spend time *organising* your data before you start. Decide *what* you want to store, and *what* you want to do with it. Work out what *fields* are required (for sorting and searching).

You can edit the structure of your table if necessary - but hunting through existing data to update records is time consuming, so it's best to get it right to start with!

Getting into Access

It is assumed that Access is already installed on your computer. If it isn't, you must install it (or get someone else to install it for you) before going any further.

● If you are already working in Windows, save any files that you want to keep, close the application(s) you are working in and return to the Desktop.

● If you are not working in Windows, switch on your computer (if necessary) and go into Windows.

You're now ready to start using Access.

You can start Access through the Start Menu on the Taskbar or from the Microsoft Office Shortcut Bar (if you have it displayed).

❑ From the Taskbar

1 Click the **Start** button on the **Taskbar.**

2 Point to **Programs.**

3 Click on **Microsoft Access.**

4 Select **Blank Database.**

5 Click [OK].

❑ From the Microsoft Office Shortcut Bar

1 Click the **Microsoft Access** tool 🔍.

2 Complete steps 4 and 5 above.

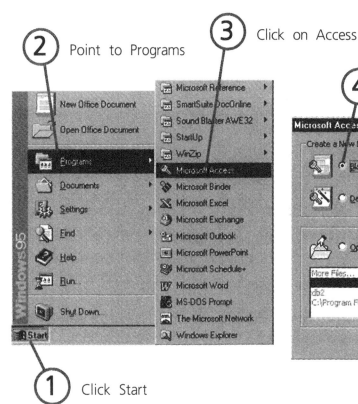

② Point to Programs

③ Click on Access

④ Select Blank Database

① Click Start

⑤ Click OK

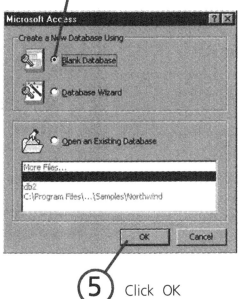

The Access screen

Close the File New Database dialog box (click Cancel), so that you can view the Microsoft Access screen.

Looking at the Access screen, you can identify the standard elements of any Window: the Title bar, Menu bar and Toolbar; the Minimize, Maximize/Restore and Close buttons, and the Status bar.

I suggest you Maximize the Access application window. This way other windows that may be open on your desktop won't distract you.

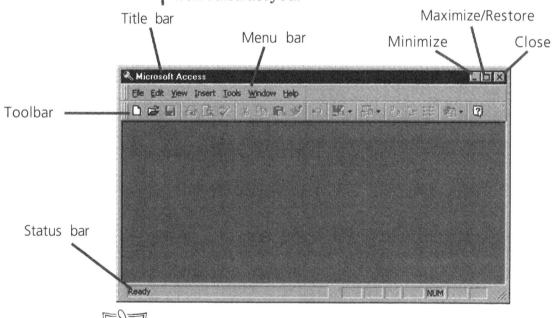

Title bar

Menu bar

Maximize/Restore

Minimize

Close

Toolbar

Status bar

Basic steps

1 Click the **Close** button ⊠ on the Title Bar.

or

2 Open the **File** menu and choose **Exit**.

Exiting Access

When you have completed your session in Access, you must exit the package and return to the Windows environment (*don't* just switch off your computer!!). To exit the package, use one of the methods suggested.

Summary

- A **database** is a collection of data.

- Access is a **relational** database.

- In a **relational database**, all related data is stored in one place.

- A relational database is organised into **tables**, **records** and **fields**.

- In Access, you will encounter various objects – **tables**, **queries**, **forms**, **reports**, **macros** and **modules**.

- **Preparation** is the first, very important step, in setting up your database.

- To **get into Access**, click **Start**, **Programs**, **Microsoft Access**.

- To get out of **Access**, click the **Close** button on the Application window, or choose **Exit** from the **File** menu.

2 Help

Office Assistant

When working in the Windows environment there is always plenty of help available—in books, in manuals, in magazines and on-line. The trick is being able to find the help you need, when you need it. In this section, we look at the various ways you can interrogate the on-line Help when you discover you're in need of it.

One of the first things you'll notice when working with any of the Office 97 applications is the 'Office Assistant'. This new interface to the on-line help system is unique and replaces the Answer Wizard found in Office 95. The Office Assistant displays help topics and tips to help you accomplish your tasks. It interacts with you through its 'dialog bubble', rather than a standard dialog box!

Basic steps

1 To display the Office Assistant press [F1].

or

Click the Office Assistant tool.

2 Click an item in the list for help on that topic.

or

3 Type in your question and click (● **Search**).

4 The Help topic(s) will appear on your screen.

5 To close the on-line help click the Close ☒ button at the top right of the Help window.

6 To close the Office Assistant, click the Close ☒ button on its title bar.

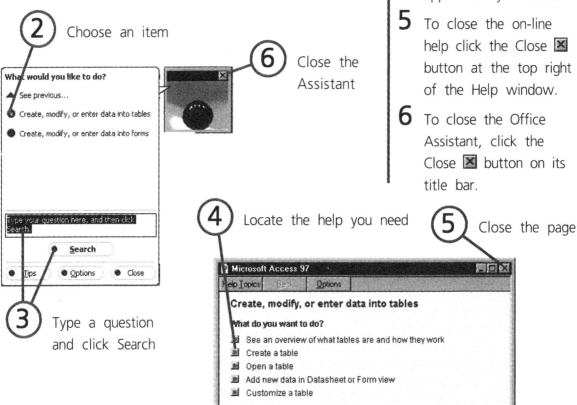

② Choose an item

⑥ Close the Assistant

What would you like to do?

▲ See previous...

● Create, modify, or enter data into tables

● Create, modify, or enter data into forms

Type your question here, and then click Search

Search

● Tips   ● Options   ● Close

③ Type a question and click Search

④ Locate the help you need

⑤ Close the page

Microsoft Access 97

Help Topics   Back   Options

Create, modify, or enter data into tables

What do you want to do?

See an overview of what tables are and how they work

Create a table

Open a table

Add new data in Datasheet or Form view

Customize a table

Basic steps

❏ **Tip of the day**

1 If you have closed the Office Assistant, display it – click 🔲.

2 Click the Tips button (● Tips). The Office Assistant will display its 'Tip of the day'.

3 Click (● Next) to display the next tip, or (● Back) to go back to the previous tip (if either option is dimmed, you are either at the beginning or the end of the list of tips).

4 When you've finished viewing the tips, click (● Close).

You may keep the Office Assistant open while you work – you can drag it (using the title bar on the Office Assistant) to a suitable area of the screen (one that doesn't obscure what you are working on) and leave it there.

To display its list of help options (which vary depending on what you are doing), or to type in a question, simply give it a click!

Big Brother is watching you!

The Office Assistant is constantly monitoring your actions. If you perform an action that there is a useful shortcut for, or a quick alternative method of doing, the Office Assistant lights up to indicate that it has a tip that you may find useful.

Click the light bulb to display the tip.

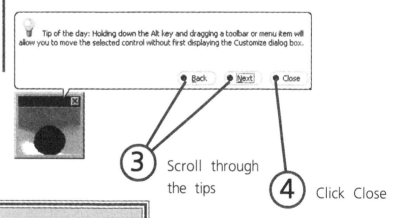

③ Scroll through the tips

④ Click Close

Tip

The Office Assistant can give you tips on features that are available to you in Access. Many of the tips give you short cuts on how to perform particular tasks.

Customising the Office Assistant

You can customise the Office Assistant to take on a different appearance or to behave in the way you find most useful.

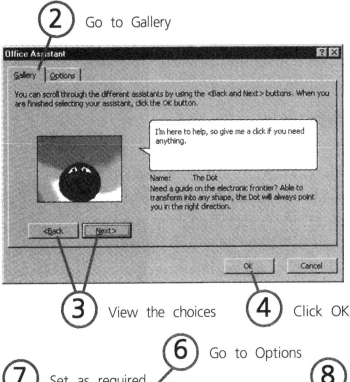

② Go to Gallery

③ View the choices

④ Click OK

⑥ Go to Options

⑦ Set as required

⑧ Click OK

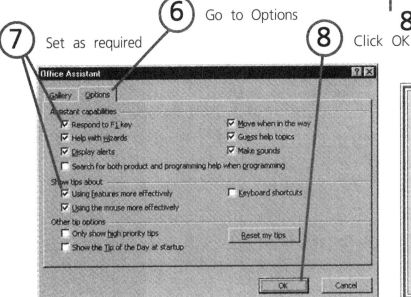

❏ **Appearance**

1 Click ⟨Options⟩ in the Assistant's bubble.

2 Select the **Gallery** tab.

3 Use ⟨Next>⟩ and ⟨<Back⟩ to see the personalities.

4 Click ⟨OK⟩ when you find the one that you want to use.

❏ **Other options**

5 Click ⟨Options⟩.

6 Select the **Options** tab.

7 Click the checkboxes to select or deselect the options as required.

8 Click ⟨OK⟩.

Take note

If you leave the Office Assistant open while you work, ⟨Options⟩ is dimmed when you are in some dialog boxes e.g. Open.

Basic steps

1 Hold down the [Shift] key and press [F1].

The mouse pointer looks like this ▶?.

❑ **To find out what a particular tool does**

2 Click the tool.

or

❑ **To find out about an item in a menu list**

3 Open the menu list by clicking on the menu name.

4 Click on the option required on the menu.

or

❑ **To find out about anything else within the application window**

5 Just click on it.

What's This?

If you are new to Microsoft Office applications or to the Windows interface, there will be many things on your screen that puzzle you at first.

There may be strange looking tools on the toolbars; items listed in the menus may suggest things you've never heard of and other objects that appear and disappear as you work may add to your confusion!

Don't panic! If you don't know what it is – ask!

② Click on a tool

Help on Spelling tool

Spelling (Tools menu)
Checks the spelling of text entries in table, query, or form Datasheet view or selected text in a text box in Form view.

③ Open a menu

④ Select an option

Tools
Spelling... F7
AutoCorrect...
Office Links
Relationships...
Analyze
Database Utilities
Security
Replication
Startup...
Macro
ActiveX Controls...
Add-Ins
Options...

AutoCorrect (Tools menu)
Customizes the settings used to automatically correct text as you type, and creates and modifies the list of words to correct as you type.

Help on AutoCorrect

Help on the New button

New button
Creates a database object. Before clicking this button, click the tab for the type of database object you want to create.

ScreenTips

If you point to any tool on a displayed toolbar, a ScreenTip appears to describe the function of the tool.

If you like using keyboard shortcuts, you can customise the ScreenTips to display the shortcut as well. This will help you learn the shortcuts quickly.

(6) Shortcut keys are displayed

You can have large icons if they will help

(3) Go to Options

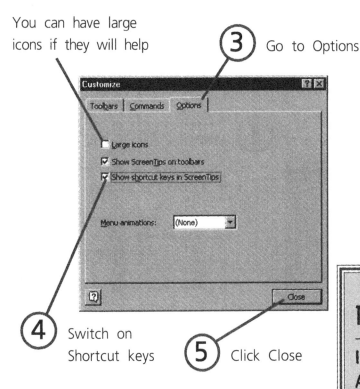

(4) Switch on Shortcut keys

(5) Click Close

☐ **To customise the ScreenTips**

1 Point to any toolbar that is displayed and click the right mouse button.

2 Choose **Customize...** from the shortcut menu.

3 Select the **Options** tab in the **Customize** dialog box.

4 Select the **Show shortcut keys in ScreenTips** option.

5 Click **Close**.

6 Point to a tool on the toolbar – if it has a shortcut key it will be displayed with the screen tip.

Take note

If you've used previous versions of Access, take a look through **Welcome to Microsoft Access 97 - What's New** on the Contents tab in the on-line Help.

Basic steps

1 Open the **Help** menu and choose **Contents and Index**.

2 At the **Help Topics** dialog box, select the **Contents** tab.

3 Select a book and click ▐ Open ▐. You may see more books, a list of topics, or both. Open the books as needed.

4 To open a topic, select it and click ▐ Display ▐.

5 Work through the Help system until you find the help you need.

6 Close the Help system.

Tip

Double click on a book to open it. Double click on a topic to display its contents.

The Help menu

The Help system can also be accessed through the Help menu. Almost everything you'll ever need to know will be somewhere in these Help pages. The Help pages can be located from the Contents, Index or Find tabs.

Contents tab

The Contents tab is a good place to 'browse'. Look through the topics and explore any that appeal to you.

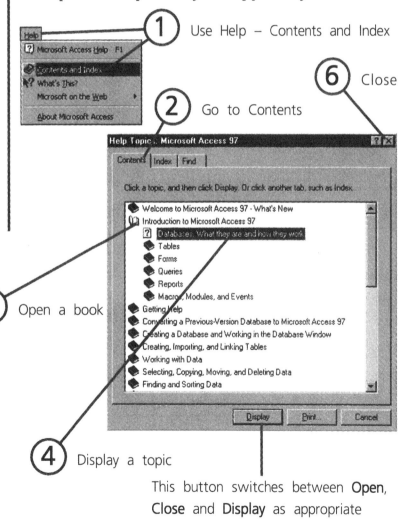

① Use Help – Contents and Index

⑥ Close

② Go to Contents

③ Open a book

④ Display a topic

This button switches between **Open**, **Close** and **Display** as appropriate

17

Index tab

The Index tab gives you quick access to any topic and is particularly useful if you know what you are looking for!

Go to Index

Start to type a word

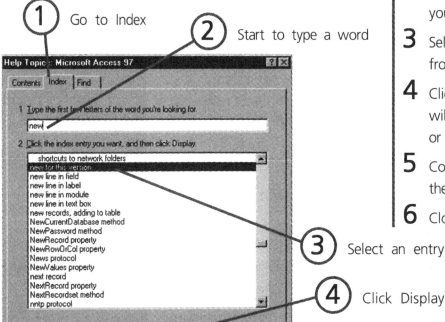

Select an entry

Click Display

Basic steps

1 Open the **Index** tab.

2 Start typing the word you're looking for.

3 Select an index entry from the list.

4 Click Display. You will see a list of topics or a Help page.

5 Continue until you find the help you need.

6 Close the Help system.

Go to the Help Topics dialog box

Back to the previous page

Options include one to print the topic

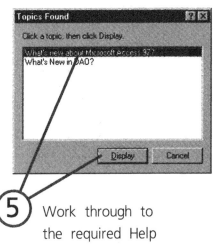

Work through to the required Help

18

Basic steps

Find tab

1 Select the **Find** tab.

2 Type in your word (or part of it – enough to get some matching words displayed).

3 Select a matching word to narrow the search.

4 Choose a topic.

5 Click [Display].

6 Close the Help when you are done.

The first time you use the Find tab, the Find Setup Wizard runs to set up your word list – just follow the prompts.

Use the Find tab to search out specific words and phrases, rather than look for a particular category of information.

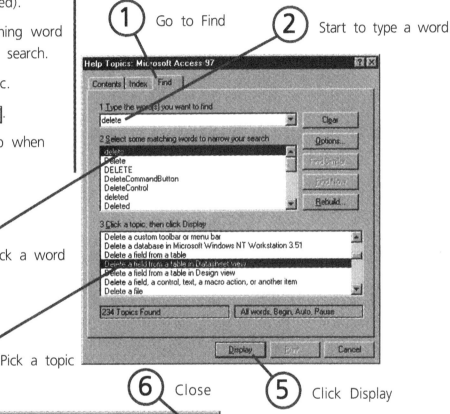

① Go to Find

② Start to type a word

③ Pick a word

④ Pick a topic

⑥ Close

⑤ Click Display

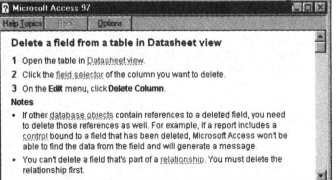

Delete a field from a table in Datasheet view

1 Open the table in Datasheet view.

2 Click the field selector of the column you want to delete.

3 On the **Edit** menu, click **Delete Column**.

Notes

• If other database objects contain references to a deleted field, you need to delete those references as well. For example, if a report includes a control bound to a field that has been deleted, Microsoft Access won't be able to find the data from the field and will generate a message.

• You can't delete a field that's part of a relationship. You must delete the relationship first.

Tip

This option is not the easiest way to get help if you're new to Access. It can be difficult to find help on 'simple' things!

Summary

❑ Press **[F1]** or click the Office Assistant tool to get help with your tasks.

❑ **What's This?** [Shift]-[F1] and click on a tool or menu item to find out.

❑ **ScreenTips** are useful learning aids when you start out using Access.

❑ Choose **Contents and Index** from the Help menu and browse through the on-line help pages from the Contents tab.

❑ Search for specific categories of information from the **Index** tab.

❑ Locate help on specific words using the **Find** tab.

3 Building a database

Creating a new database

The first thing we have to do is create a database for our data, and give the database a suitable name.

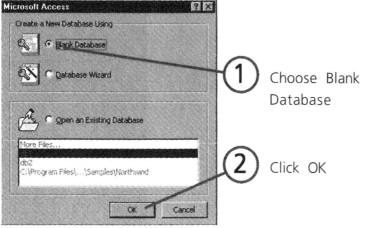

(1) Choose Blank Database

(2) Click OK

(5) Select the folder

(8) Click Create

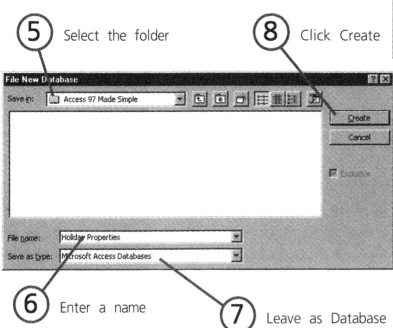

(6) Enter a name

(7) Leave as Database

❏ **On starting Access**

1 Choose **Blank Database** at the **Microsoft Access** dialog box.

2 Click [OK].

❏ **From within Access**

3 Open the **File** menu and choose **New Database** or click 🗋.

4 Choose **Blank Database** from the **General Tab** and click [OK].

5 Select the folder.

6 At the **File New Database**, enter a **File name**. Here it is called *Holiday Properties*.

7 Leave the **Save as type:** field at **Microsoft Access Databases**.

8 Click [Create].

The project

The next sections describe a project that you may like to work through. It demonstrates many of the Access features you need to get to grips with.

You have set up a travel service that has an extensive database of quality accommodation.

Your clients will contact you with details of:

● where they want to go;
● when they want to go;
● how many people need to be accommodated;
● what kind of board, e.g. self-catering, is required.

You can then interrogate your database to get a list of properties that match their requirements and check prices. If a client decides to make a booking, you can get the name, address and telephone number of the property's owners, and contact them to arrange the let.

Your Holiday Database will consist of four tables:

● **Type of Accommodation** eg cottage, flat, apartment or room;
● **Accommodation details,** e.g. location, number of beds, whether it has a garden/pool/maid service;
● one with **Price** details;
● one with details of the property owner or **Contact.**

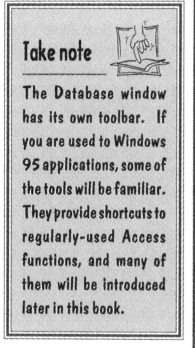

Take note

The Database window has its own toolbar. If you are used to Windows 95 applications, some of the tools will be familiar. They provide shortcuts to regularly-used Access functions, and many of them will be introduced later in this book.

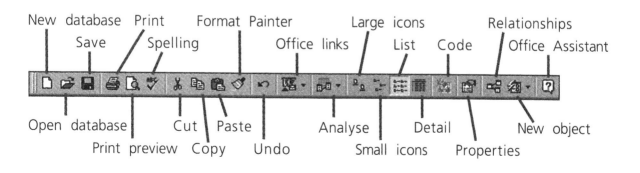

New database | Print | Format Painter | Large icons | Relationships
Save | Spelling | Office links | List | Code | Office Assistant

Open database | Cut | Paste | Analyse | Detail | New object
Print preview | Copy | Undo | Small icons | Properties

Creating a new table

The data you store will be held in a table (or tables). A table consists of:

- the record **structure**, that is, the field names, data types, dDescriptions and field properties;

and

- the record **detail**, for example, accommodation details, price details, contact details.

Give careful consideration to your table structure. It can be edited (you can add fields, delete fields and change the field properties) at a later stage, but things are a lot easier if you get it right to begin with.

You must decide:

- what **fields** you require in your table;

- what kind of data will go in each field, ie text, date, number, etc.;

- which field will be your **key field** – one that uniquely identifies the record, e.g. property code, product code, employeer reference number.

Once you've worked out the structure, you can then create your table.

Basic steps

1 Ensure the **Tables** object tab is selected in your database window.

2 Choose **New**.

3 At the **New Table** dialog box, choose **Design View**.

4 Click [OK].

Tip

Good planning at the start is the secret of good databases. Be clear about what you want to store and what you intend to do with the data once it's stored.

Take note

You can also create a new table if you click the drop down arrow beside the **New Object** tool on the Database window Toolbar and choose **Table**.

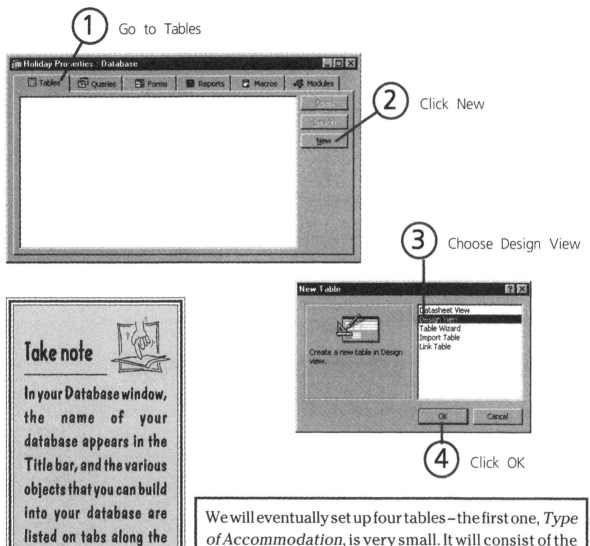

① Go to Tables

② Click New

③ Choose Design View

④ Click OK

Take note

In your Database window, the name of your database appears in the Title bar, and the various objects that you can build into your database are listed on tabs along the top of the window.

We will eventually set up four tables – the first one, *Type of Accommodation*, is very small. It will consist of the type of accommodation code, and its full description. The accommodation may be an apartment (code 1), a cottage (code 2), a flat (code 3) or a room (code 4). This table must set up before the *Accommodation* table. The *Accommodation* table will eventually hold the type of accommodation code, which will be used to look up the full description in the *Type of Accommodation* table.

Table Design window

The Table Design window has two panes – one that lets you specify the field name, data type and description, and the other where you can specify the field properties.

You can use the **Field Properties** pane to customise the format of the field you are defining. The amount of customisation permitted depends on the data type selected for the field, for example:

- the number of characters in a Text field;
- the format of the date in a Date/Time field;
- the decimal accuracy of a Number field;
- whether Duplicate entries are permitted in a field.

We'll consider some of the properties in the next pages.

Take note

Table Design has its own toolbar. You have met some of these already; others will be introduced in the next few sections.

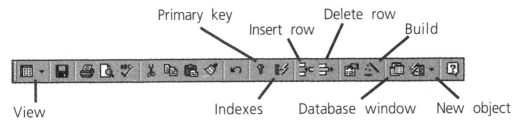

View   Primary key   Insert row   Delete row   Build   Indexes   Database window   New object

Type of Accommodation table

The first table we will create will holds details of the accommodation type – its code and description. This detail will be looked up from the *Accommodation* table.

Detail on the structure of the table is given below:

Field Name	Data Type	Format /Field size	Other field properties/Notes
AccCode	Number	Long Integer	Primary key
Description	Text	20	

Take note

Any table storing data that will be looked up by another table must be set up *before* the one that will do the looking up.

26

Basic steps

1 Type in the first **Field Name** in your table – *AccCode*.

2 Press **[Tab]**, or point and click, to move to the **Data Type**.

3 Click the down arrow to display the list of data types.

4 Choose the type – **Number** in this case.

5 In the **Description** column, type in the message to be shown in the Status bar when data is entered in this field. If you don't want a message, leave it blank.

6 Press **[Tab]** to move to the Field Name column for your next field.

Number data type

In a field with a **Number** data type, you can specify the accuracy of the number that can be entered by setting the **Field Size** property. For the *AccCode* field leave the Field Size at the default – Long Integer. This table will eventually be related to the *Accommodation* table through this field.

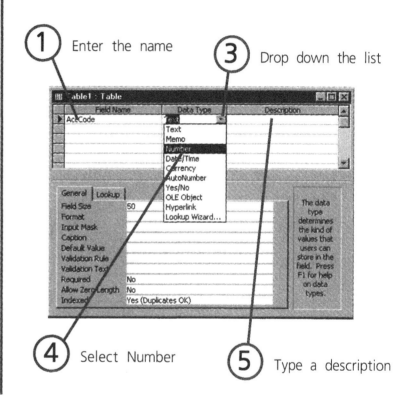

① Enter the name

③ Drop down the list

④ Select Number

⑤ Type a description

Take note

Field names can be up to **64 characters** in length and can include any combination of text, numbers, spaces and special characters, except for the period (.), exclamation mark (!), accent grave (') and square brackets ([ ]).

Text data type

The next field is the accommodation description field. This field is a text field that will hold the accommodation description – apartment, cottage, flat or room. 20 characters will be more than long enough for this field.

The Field Size is set in the **Field Properties** pane. Pressing [F6] switches between the upper and lower panes.

1 Type in the **Field Name** – *Description*.

2 Set the **Data Type** to **Text**.

3 Enter a **Description** if you wish.

4 Press **[F6]** to move to the lower pane.

5 Change the **Field Size** property to 20.

6 Press **[F6]** to return to the upper pane.

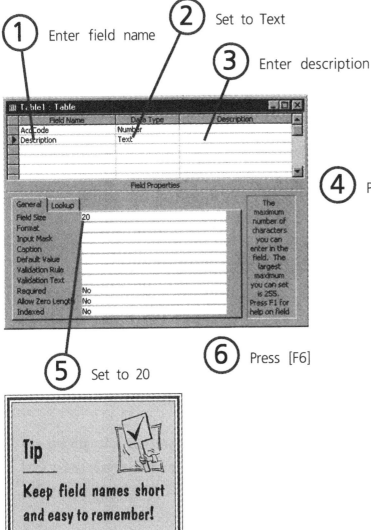

① Enter field name

② Set to Text

③ Enter description

④ Press [F6]

⑤ Set to 20

⑥ Press [F6]

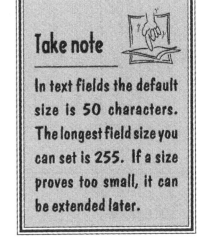

Tip

Keep field names short and easy to remember!

Take note

In text fields the default size is 50 characters. The longest field size you can set is 255. If a size proves too small, it can be extended later.

Basic steps

1 To select a single field to become your primary key, click anywhere inside the field row in the upper pane.

2 Click the **primary key** tool on the toolbar.

❏ Note the key icon that appears to the left of the key field(s).

Primary key

Once you have completed specifying your table structure, and edited any fields you want to change, you should indicate which field is to be your primary key. The primary key is a field (or combination of fields) that uniquely identifies each record in your table.

If you don't specify the primary key, Access can set one up when you first save your design. It will set up a field called *ID* with an AutoNumber data type if you do this.

We will specify the *AccCode* field as our Primary key.

① Select the field

Key icon

Take note

The Primary key tool is a toggle switch — it adds or removes primary key status to or from the selected field.

Take note

To select several fields to become your primary key, hold the [Ctrl] key down as you click the row selector bar — the grey bar down the left-hand side of the field names for each field.

If you choose the wrong field (or fields) to be your primary key, simply select the correct one (or ones) and click the primary key tool.

29

Saving the design

When you have the table design specified, you must **save** it. Once the design has been saved, you can:

- Close the table (and the database) and leave data entry till later;

or

- Move into the Datasheet View, so you can enter data straight away (see Chapter 6).

At this stage, I suggest you close the Datasheet and leave data entry for Chapter 6.

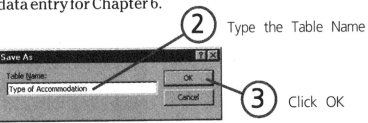

Type the Table Name

Click OK

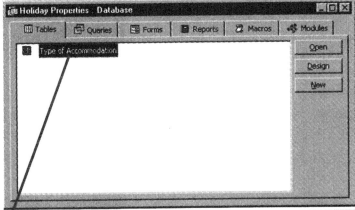

The new table is listed

Click View tool

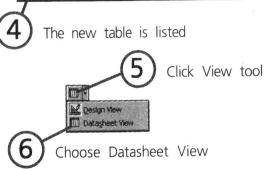

Choose Datasheet View

Basic steps

1 Click the **Save** tool.

2 At the **Save As** dialog box, enter *Type of Accommodation* as the **Table Name**.

3 Click OK.

❑ **Enter data later**

4 Click ☒ to close the Design window. At the Database window the new table is listed on the Tables tab.

❑ **Go to Datasheet View**

5 Click the **View** tool on the Toolbar.

or

6 Click the arrow beside the **View** tool and choose **Datasheet View**. You arrive in Datasheet View ready for data entry.

Take note

Once your table design has been saved, clicking the Save tool 🖫 will record to disk any changes you make.

30

Closing a database

1 Click the Close button 🗵 on the Database window.

❑ Your database is closed, but you are still in Access.

If you've finished working on your database, you might want to close it. You can close a database without leaving Access. If you exit Access, any open databases are closed as part of the exit routine.

 Close the database

Take note

You can't exit from the Design View without being reminded to save your design if you haven't already done so.

If you don't want to save, choose NO at the *Must save changes* first, or *Save changes?* prompts, that appear.

Tip

Save your table design regularly as you work (this is particularly important with larger tables) – don't leave it till the end.

If there's a power failure, or your computer crashes and the design hasn't been saved, it will be lost and you'll have to start all over again.

If you save regularly and such a disaster befalls you, at least you'll have the design as it was at the last save.

Summary

- ❑ To create a **new database,** click the New Database tool 🗋 on the Database toolbar.

- ❑ To create a **new table,** select the Tables tab on the Database window and click New.

- ❑ Each field *must* have a **Field Name** and a **Data Type.**

- ❑ Each table should have a unique field (or fields) set as the **primary key.**

- ❑ You should **save your table** design regularly as you build it up (click the Save tool 🖫 on the Design toolbar).

- ❑ To close your table design and return to the Database window, click the Close button ⊠.

- ❑ To change from **Design** View to **Datasheet** View in your Table, click the **View** tool ▦.

- ❑ **Number** and **Text** data types are introduced in this section.

- ❑ To **close a database**, but remain in Access, click the close button on the Database window.

32

4 Data types

Opening a database

If the database you want to work on exists, but is not open, you must open it before you can work on it.

If you closed your database at the end of the last section, you will need to open it again before you can set up the final table and the relationships in this section.

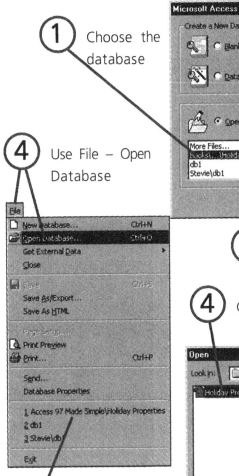

① Choose the database

④ Use File – Open Database

② Click OK

Recently used files are listed at the end of the File menu. Just click to open one of these.

❑ As you go into Access

1 Select the Database from the **Microsoft Access** dialog box.

2 Click ⬚ OK ⬚.

❑ **From within Access**

3 Click the **Open Database** tool 🖼.

Or

4 Choose **Open Database** from the **File** menu.

5 At the **Open** dialog box, choose the database.

6 Click ⬚ Open ⬚ or double-click on it.

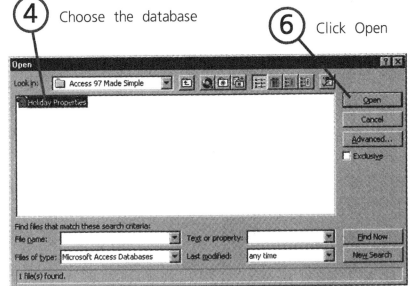

④ Choose the database

⑥ Click Open

34

Adding a new table

Create a new table as shown on page 24, then move to the Table Design window to define the first field.

This next table is much larger than the previous one, and needs to use many different data types in its structure. A summary of the fields and their properties is shown below/opposite. Full instructions will be given to help you set up each new data type. Check the data types and properties of the fields overleaf to help you complete the table accurately.

Accommodation table

The *Accommodation* table will hold details of the holiday accommodation we have on offer.

- Board is self-catering (SC), bed and breakfast (BB) or half board (HB).

- Properties may have a swimming pool, maid service or garden.

- Prices depend on the time of year.

- The type of accommodation - apartment (1), cottage (2), flat (3) or room (4) will be 'looked up' in the *Type of Accommodation* table.

- A photograph of the accommodation will be included in this table.

- Information files on the general area surrounding our properties, e.g. places to visit, good eating and drinking houses have been keyed into Word documents.

- We will set up a 'hyperlink' field in this table to link to these files as appropriate.

Accommodation table

Field Name	Data Type	Format/Field size	Other field properties/Notes
Reference	AutoNumber		Primary Key.Indexed (No Duplicates)
Season Start	Date/Time	Short date	Input Mask 99/99/00
Season End	Date/Time	Short date	Input Mask 99/99/00
Country	Text	20	Indexed
Board	Text	2	Validation rule ="SC" or ="BB" or ="HB"
AccCode	Lookup		
Swimming Pool	Yes/No	Yes/No	
Maid Service	Yes/No	Yes/No	Default Value = Yes
Garden	Yes/No	Yes/No	
Price Range	Text	1	Description: Enter Code A-E Validation rule ="A" or ="B" or ="C" or ="D" or ="E"
Sleeps	Number	Integer	Default Value = 4
ContactID	Number	Long integer	Required = YES
Notes	Memo		For information specific to the property, but not covered by the other fields
Picture	OLE Object		For a photograph of the property
General Information	Hyperlink		To link to Word documents containing background information

Take note

For Input Mask – see page 40
For Validation rule – see page 42

Basic steps

1 Type in the first **Field Name**.

2 Choose **AutoNumber** in the **Data Type** column.

3 Enter a **Description** if you wish.

4 Make this field your **primary key** – click 🔑.

5 Press **[Tab]** to move to the **Field Name** column for your next field.

AutoNumber

Our first field will contain the accommodation reference. This will be the unique identifier for each property – no two will have the same reference. The field could be called something like *Reference* or *Accommodation Code*.

Fields that are used as identification fields in this way can be completed automatically by Access if the reference field is given an **AutoNumber** data type. When you enter data into the finished table, Access puts 1 in the *Reference* field in the first record, 2 in the second, 3 in the third and so on. You *cannot* enter data into the field, and Access never uses the same number twice (even if records are added and deleted later), so the field is always unique.

Take note

When specifying a field's properties, ensure that your insertion point is inside the correct Field in the upper pane, before you press [F6] to move to the lower pane. The current field is clearly indicated by the black triangle in the selector column, to the left of the field name.

① Enter field name

② Choose AutoNumber

③ Description wanted?

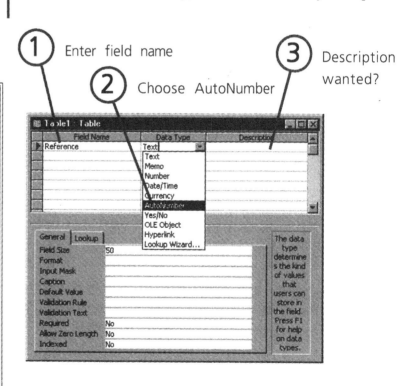

With an AutoNumber data type, you can specify up to five field properties (see next page).

Field size

Use the smallest practical field size. Smaller sizes can be processed faster and require less memory. Long Integer is the smallest option for the AutoNumber data type.

New values

Leave this set at *Increment* to have the reference automatically incremented by 1 at each new record.

Format

You can specify the number format for the AutoNumber field. You can select the from the drop-down list of pre-set formats, or specify your own format.

To define a format, key the number pattern into the Format field. Characters that can be used include:

0	a digit or 0	.	the decimal separator
#	a digit or nothing	""	a literal (something that actually appears in the field)

Other permitted user characters are listed in the on-line Help under **Format Property**.

Caption

In the Caption field, you can type the label to appear beside the field when it is inserted into a **form**. (We will deal with forms in Chapter 10.) A caption can be more user-friendly than a field name. If we use a field name like *Ref*, a suitable Caption might be 'Accommodation Code'.

Indexed

Indexing fields can speed up searches (although updates are slower). If a field is designated the **Primary Key** this property is automatically set to *Yes, (No Duplicates)*.

Take note

The Format property option also appears in fields that have a Text data type.

The Caption property option is present for all data types.

The Indexed property option is present for all data types except Memo, OLE and Hyperlink.

Indexed fields have either 'No Duplicates' or 'Duplicates OK' status. 'No Duplicates' ensures that the value in the field is unique. 'Duplicates OK' allows non-unique values to be entered.

Basic steps

1 Type *Season Start* as the **Field Name**.

2 For the **Data Type** select **Date/Time**.

3 Press **[F6]** to switch to the **Field Properties** pane.

4 Click the drop-down arrow to display the list of **Format** options.

5 Choose **Short Date**.

6 Press **[F6]** to return to the upper pane.

7 Key in a **Description** if required (e.g. *Only needed if not open all year*).

❑ Set up the *Season End* field in the same way.

Date/Time

At our *Season Start* and *Season End* fields we are going to specify a Date/Time data type.

We will specify the format the date will take as DD/MM/YY (e.g. 01/06/97) – what Access calls a Short Date format. This is specified in the Field Properties pane.

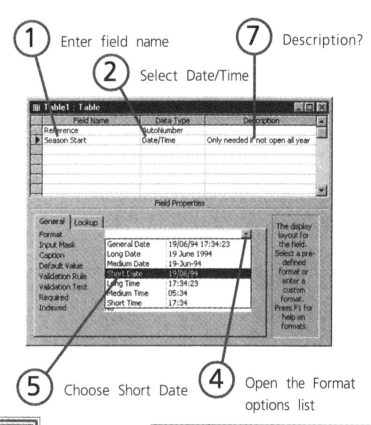

① Enter field name ⑦ Description?

② Select Date/Time

⑤ Choose Short Date ④ Open the Format options list

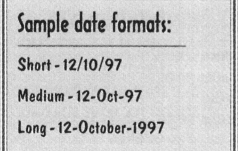

Sample date formats:

Short - 12/10/97

Medium - 12-Oct-97

Long - 12-October-1997

Take note

Date formats follow the Regional Setting Properties specified in the Control Panel in Windows 95.

Input Mask

Regardless of how you choose to display your date, you will want to make sure that the date is keyed in accurately.

Different people might key in the same date with different separators between the day, month and year. 12/06/97, 12:06:97, 12-06-97 or 12.06.97 may all mean the 12th of June 1997 to us, but Access might not be so sure! To help ensure that data entry is completed correctly, you can specify an Input Mask, or pattern, the data should take.

● The Input Mask does not affect the display Format.

Go back to the *Season Start* field to set up an Input Mask.

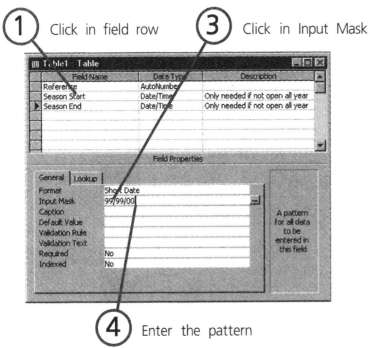

Click in field row ③ Click in Input Mask

④ Enter the pattern

● When you enter data into these fields, an underscore will appear to indicate the position for each digit, and the slash character will be in place between the day, month and year sections (__/__/__) – it will not be necessary to key in the slash at data entry.

Basic steps

1 Put the insertion point in the *Season Start* field in the upper pane.

2 Press [F6] to move to the lower pane.

3 Move to the **Input Mask** field.

4 Key in the pattern 99/99/00 (see table opposite).

5 Press [F6] to return to the upper pane.

❑ Do the same for the *Season End* field.

Tip

You can use a Wizard to help you build your Input Mask. To try it, click the Build button ▣ to the right of the Input Mask property field. If you use the Wizard, all three parts of the Input Mask are specified.

Input Mask patterns

When setting up your pattern, you use special characters to show the type of input allowed, and whether or not input is required. These are listed here.

0	Digit (0-9). Entry required. Plus (+) and Minus (-) signs not allowed.
9	Digit or space. Entry not required. Plus and Minus signs not allowed.
#	Digit or space. Entry not required. Plus and Minus signs allowed.
L	Letter (A-Z). Entry required.
?	Letter (A-Z). Entry not required.
A	Letter or digit. Entry required.
a	Letter or digit. Entry not required.
&	Any character or a space. Entry required.
C	Any character or a space. Entry not required.
<	Causes all characters that follow to be converted to lower case.
>	Causes all characters that follow to be converted to upper case.
!	Causes Input Mask to fill from right to left when characters on the left side are optional.
\	Causes the following character to be displayed as the literal character, not interpreted as a mask code character, i.e. \L is displayed as L, and doesn't mean Letter (A-Z). Entry required.

An Input Mask can contain up to three parts, each part being separated from the others using a semi-colon i.e. 99/99/00;0;_

● The first part, 99/99/00, specifies the Input Mask itself.

● The second part specifies whether any literal display characters are stored with the data. 0 means that they are; 1 means that only data is stored. The default is 0.

● The third part specifies the character used to display spaces in the Input Mask. The default character is the underline. If you want to use a space, enclose it in quotes i.e. 99/99/00;0; " "

Indexed property

As the *Country*, *Board*, *Price Range* and *Type of Accommodation* fields may be used in sorts and queries, they should be indexed with duplicates allowed.

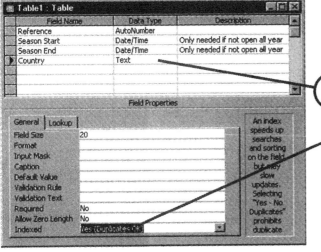

Set up the field

Choose Yes

Validation Rule property

Validation rules ensure that only the valid data is entered. The *Board* field should only accept one of these codes – SC (self-catering), BB (bed & breakfast) or HB (half board).

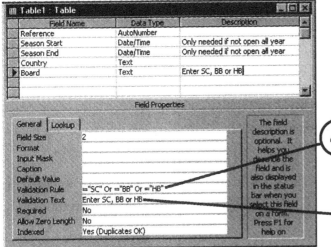

Enter Rule

Type Validation Text

Basic steps

❑ **Indexed property**

1 Set up the *Country* field as a **Text** field, setting the size to 20.

2 Set **Indexed** to **Yes** (Duplicates OK).

❑ **Validation Rule**

3 Set up the *Board* field as a text field, Size 2.

4 In the **Validation Rule** field enter = *"SC"* or = *"BB"* or = *"HB"*.

5 Type the **Validation Text** to appear if the rule is not met.

❑ Set up the *Price Range* field, Size 1, with a **Validation Rule** of = *"A"* or = *"B"* or = *"C"* or = *"D"* or = *"E"*.

Basic steps

1 Enter the **Field Name** – *AccCode.*

2 In the **Data Type** field, choose **Lookup Wizard...** Work through it, clicking [Next>] after each step and [Finish] at the end.

3 At the first step, choose *I want the lookup column to look up the values...*

4 Select the table or query that contains the data (if you're working through this project you want the *Type of Accommodation* table).

We will set up the *AccCode* as a Lookup field. The data for a Lookup field is stored in another table, and looked up as necessary. The advantages of using a Lookup field are:

● The actual data needs to be keyed in only once;

● The table receiving the data is easier to read as it contains fewer visible codes.

This field will look up the *Type of Accommodation* table for its data.

③ Take the first option

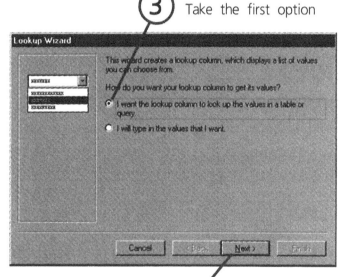

Click Next after each

④ Select the table

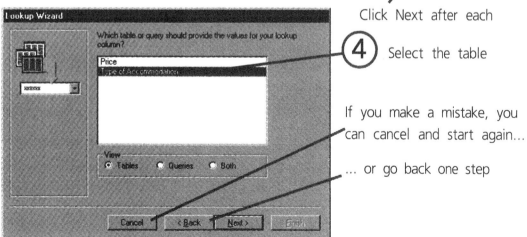

If you make a mistake, you can cancel and start again...

... or go back one step

5 Select Description

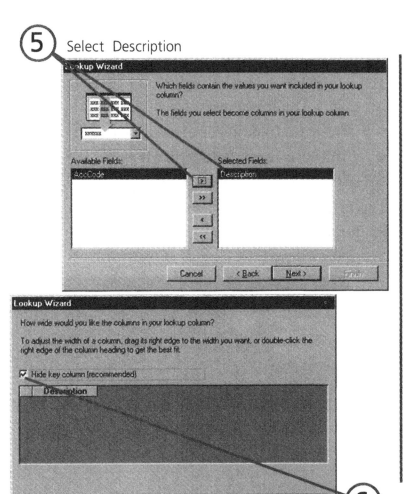

5 Select the field containing the values to be looked up – *Description* in our case.

6 Leave the **Hide key** column ticked.

7 The chequered flag marks the end! Edit the column label if you want something other than that suggested, e.g. *Type of Accommodation*.

8 When prompted to save your table, choose **Yes**. At the **Save As** dialog box, name it *Accommodation*, and click ▭ OK ▭ .

6 Tick Hide key column

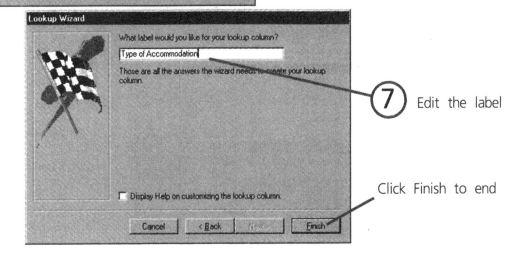

7 Edit the label

Click Finish to end

44

Basic steps

1 Type in the **Field Name** – *Swimming Pool.*

2 Set the **Data Type** to **Yes/No.**

❏ Set up the *Maid Service* and *Garden* fields in the same way.

❏ **Default value**

3 Place the insertion point in the *Maid Service* field.

4 Press **[F6]** and in the **Default Value** field, type *Yes.*

❏ Set up the *Sleeps* field with a **Number** data type and a **Default Value** of 4.

❏ **Required property**

5 Set up the *ContactID* field with a **Number** data type.

6 Press **[F6]** and set the **Field Size** to **Long Integer.**

7 Set the **Required** property option to **Yes.**

If a field can have one of two values in it, e.g. *Yes* or *No*, *True* or *False*, *On* or *Off*, choose the **Yes/No** data dype. The next three fields – Swimming Pool, Maid Service and Garden – are all Yes/No fields.

① Enter the name ② Set to Yes/No

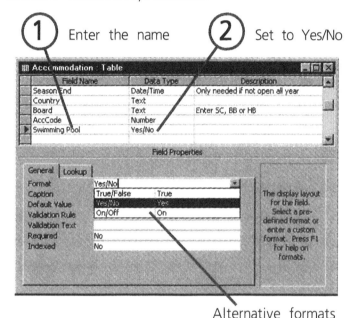

Alternative formats

Default value

The default value in a Yes/No field is *No*. As we know that most of our holiday accommodation has Maid Service, we can change the default value to *Yes* by typing *Yes* in the Default Value field of the lower pane for that field.

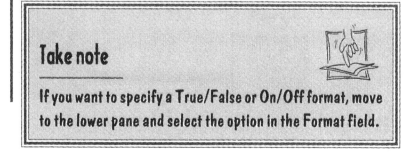

Take note

If you want to specify a True/False or On/Off format, move to the lower pane and select the option in the Format field.

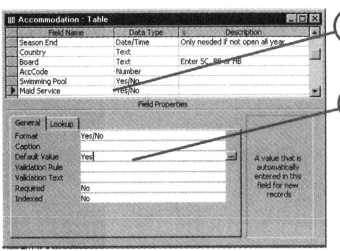

③ Click in field row

④ Set the Default Value

Required property

As the *ContactID* field will be used to link the *Accommodation* table with the *Contacts* table, we must have an entry in it. We will therefore set the **Required** field option to **Yes**.

⑤ Create the field

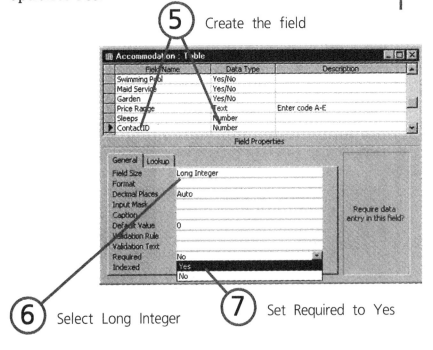

⑥ Select Long Integer

⑦ Set Required to Yes

Basic steps

1 Key in the **Field Name**.

2 Set the **Data Type** to **Memo** or to **OLE Object**.

3 Type in a **Description** if required.

Memo fields are used to add descriptive detail to your records. You can add 'unstructured' notes in a Memo field. You can't sort or search on this field type, but it's very useful for holding additional information that you feel is relevant. Any detail specific to the property, but not covered in the other fields could be included here, e.g. distance to the nearest pub, shop, etc.

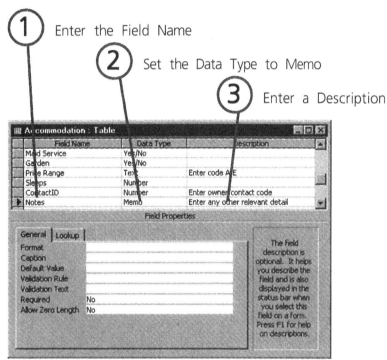

① Enter the Field Name

② Set the Data Type to Memo

③ Enter a Description

Take note

Memo fields can hold up to 65,535 characters and are mainly used for notes and comments. Memo fields cannot be indexed.

OLE Object data type

OLE stands for Object Linking and Embedding. An OLE Object is one that is created in another application that uses the OLE protocol, and is either linked to or embedded into your Access table. It may be a Word document, Excel spreadsheet, picture, sound or other binary data. In our *Accommodation* table, we could set up a field that will contain a photograph of the property we have to let.

Take note

An OLE Object can be up to 1 gigabyte in size.

Hyperlink

In our *Accommodation* table, we will set up a Hyperlink field that will access Word documents describing the surrounding area, main attractions, etc. for each property.

The data would be keyed in once – to a Word document. The Hyperlink field in our Access table would then link through to the document (several records can Hyperlink to the same document if necessary).

Using this method general background information can be stored centrally, and shared by the records.

Basic steps

1 Key in the **Field Name**.

2 Set the **Data Type** to **Hyperlink**.

3 Type in a **Description** if required.

The *Accommodation* table is now complete. Save it and close the Design window.

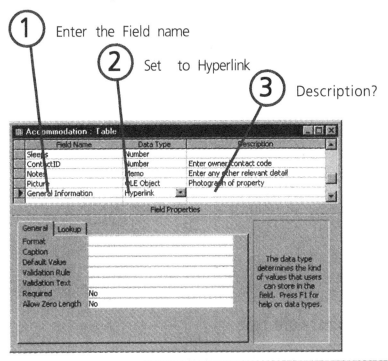

① Enter the Field name

② Set to Hyperlink

③ Description?

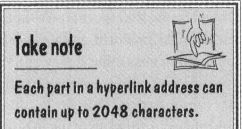

Take note

Each part in a hyperlink address can contain up to 2048 characters.

Take note

A Hyperlink field can store a UNC (Universal Naming Convention) path – the standard format for paths that include a LAN file server, or a URL (Uniform Resource Locator) – an address to an object, document, page or other destination on the Internet or on an intranet.

Basic steps

1 Set up the *Price Range* field – see the table. Make this field the **Primary Key**.

2 **[Tab]** through to the next row.

3 Key in the **Field Name** e.g. *Jan–Feb*.

4 Set the **Data Type** to **Currency**.

5 **[Tab]** through to the next row.

6 Set up the remaining fields in this way, naming them *Mar–Apr, May–Jun, Jul–Aug, Sept–Oct, Nov–Dec.*

7 Save the Table Design – table name *Price*.

8 Close the Design window and return to the Database window.

Currency

Create a new table as shown on page 24, then move to the Table Design window and define the first field.

Most of the fields in this table will hold monetary values, and should therefore have the Currency data type.

Price table

We'll set up the structure for the *Price* table next. Its fields, data types and properties are shown below.

Field name	Data type	Size	Other properties
Price Range	Text	1	Primary Key **Validation Rule** =*"A" or ="B" or ="C" or = "D" or ="E"*
Jan-Feb	Currency		
Mar-Apr	Currency		
etc			

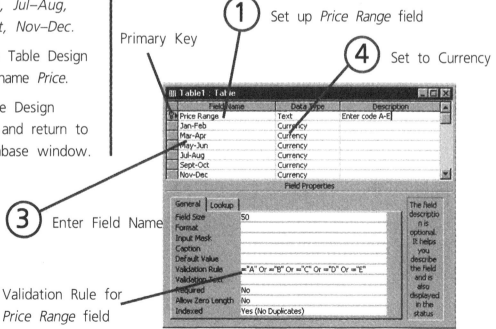

① Set up *Price Range* field

Primary Key

④ Set to Currency

③ Enter Field Name

Validation Rule for *Price Range* field

Summary

- ❏ To **open a database**, click the **Open Database** icon on the toolbar and complete the dialog box as required.

- ❏ AutoNumber, Date/Time, Lookup, Yes/No, Memo, OLE Object and Hyperlink Data Types are introduced in this section.

- ❏ For each Data Type, you can set various **Field Properties** as required.

- ❏ Use an **Input Mask** to control the pattern of data entered into a field.

- ❏ **Index** fields to speed up sort and search operations.

- ❏ If a field will have a specific value for most of the entries, set it as a **default value** in the property options.

- ❏ For fields that must have data entered, set the **Required** property to Yes.

- ❏ **Validation rules** can be set to help ensure the accuracy of data on input.

50

5 Relationships

Table Wizard

Instead of specifying your table design from scratch, you might find Table Wizard useful for some tables. We'll use it to set up our *Contacts* table for the Holiday Properties database.

Contacts table

Our final table in the Holiday Properties database is *Contacts*. This table will contain the names and addresses of the people who either own or manage the properties on our lists.

Basic steps

1 Click **New** on the **Tables** tab at the Holiday Properties database window.

2 Choose **Table Wizard**.

3 Click [OK].

4 At the **Table Wizard** dialog box, select the category of Table – in our case **Business**.

5 Choose *Contacts* from the **Sample Tables** list.

② Choose Table Wizard

③ Click OK

⑤ Select a Sample Table

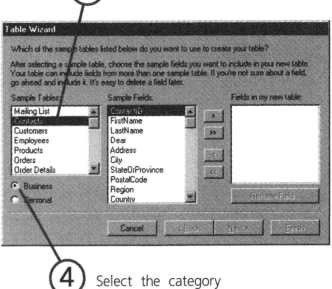

④ Select the category

52

Basic steps

1 Select the field from the **Sample Fields** list.

2 Click the **Add** field button [>] to add the field to the **Fields in my new table** list.

3 If you add a field by mistake, select it and click [<].

❏ **Renaming a field**

4 Select it and click [Rename Field...]

5 Key in the new name and click [OK]

6 Continue until you've added all the fields then click [Next>].

Specifying the fields

Using the table opposite as a guide, select the fields you want to use in your *Contacts* table. It is essentially a name and address table for our property owners/contacts.

When adding fields to the **Fields in my new table** list, the field name can be changed (e.g. *State* to *County*).

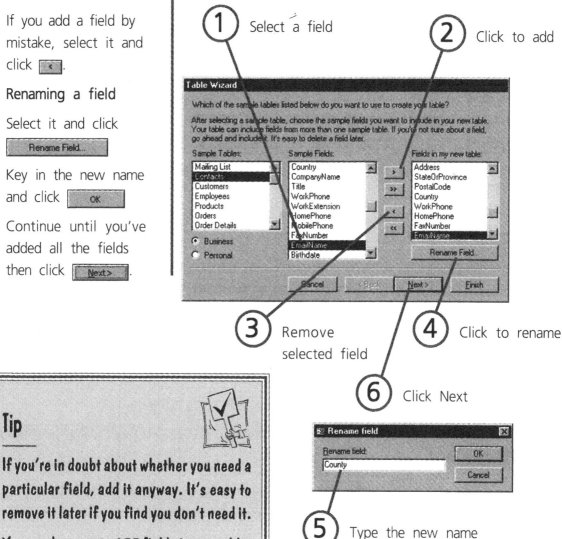

(1) Select a field

(2) Click to add

(3) Remove selected field

(4) Click to rename

(6) Click Next

(5) Type the new name

Tip

If you're in doubt about whether you need a particular field, add it anyway. It's easy to remove it later if you find you don't need it.

You can have up to 255 fields in any table.

53

Contacts table

Field Name	Notes
ContactID	Primary Key – specifying this comes AFTER the fields are set up
First name	Set up using a Table Wizard therefore field attributes picked up from Wizard
Last Name	Set up using a Table Wizard therefore field attributes picked up from Wizard
Address	Set up using a Table Wizard therefore field attributes picked up from Wizard
City	Set up using a Table Wizard therefore field attributes picked up from Wizard
State	This field name is changed to County during set up process
Postal Code	Check the field properties once the design is complete. *
Country	Set up using a Table Wizard therefore field attributes picked up from Wizard
Workphone	Check the field properties once the design is complete. *
Homephone	Check the field properties once the design is complete.*

Things like Input Masks will need to be edited or deleted as they follow the American conventions

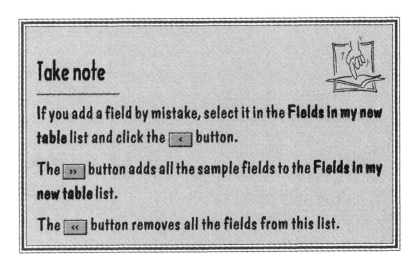

Take note

If you add a field by mistake, select it in the **Fields in my new table** list and click the [<] button.

The [»] button adds all the sample fields to the **Fields in my new table** list.

The [«] button removes all the fields from this list.

Basic steps

Finishing off

1 Edit the table name if necessary.

2 Specify whether Access or you will set the primary key. Leave it to Access – it sets the *ContactID* field as the primary key, with an AutoNumber data type.

3 Click [Next>].

Once you have specified the field names for your table, the next step is to name the table and set the Primary Key.

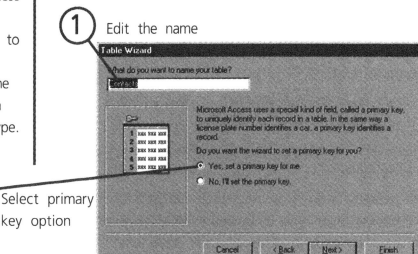

① Edit the name

② Select primary key option

Take note

ContactID in the *Contacts* and the *Accommodation* tables will be the fields through which these tables are related. You can make this relationship at the end.

Take note

If you choose No I'll set the primary key, then click Next, Access requests additional information about the type of data the primary key will hold.

Checking relationships

Normally, if a database contains more than one table, each table is related to at least one other. In our *Accommodation* table there is a *ContactID* field, which holds the code of the contact. In the *Contacts* table, there is also a *ContactID* field (set as the primary key) that will hold the same code. The two are related through this common field.

Table Wizard displays a list of the tables in your database, and indicates whether or not they are related. (In some cases the Wizard makes the relationship between tables automatically.)

You must check the relationships, and edit if necessary. In this example, you will need to set the relationship between the *Accommodation* and *Contacts* tables.

① Select the table

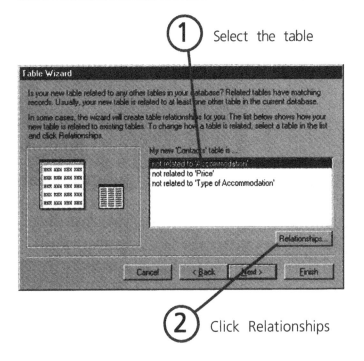

② Click Relationships

Basic steps

1 Select the table with the relationship you want to check or change.

2 Click [Relationships...].

3 The current type of relationship is shown in the **Relationships** dialog box. Select the *One record will match many...* option. One Contact or owner may have several holiday properties in our *Accommodation* table.

4 Click [OK].

5 Once you are satisfied that the relationships are OK, click [Next>].

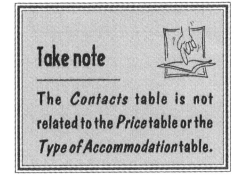

Take note

The *Contacts* table is not related to the *Price* table or the *Type of Accommodation* table.

56

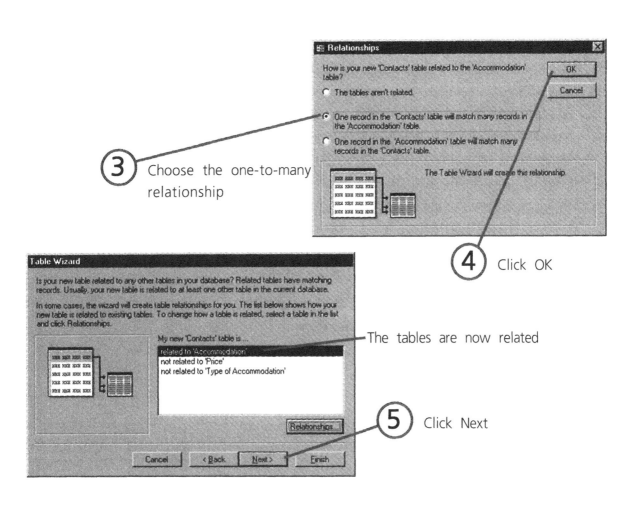

③ Choose the one-to-many relationship

④ Click OK

The tables are now related

⑤ Click Next

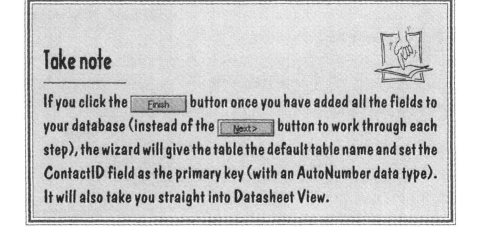

Take note

If you click the [Finish] button once you have added all the fields to your database (instead of the [Next>] button to work through each step), the wizard will give the table the default table name and set the ContactID field as the primary key (with an AutoNumber data type). It will also take you straight into Datasheet View.

Leaving Table Wizard

The last step is to choose where to go next.

- **Modify the table design** takes you to the Design window to modify the structure. We need to do this. *Postal Code*, *WorkPhone* and *HomePhone* fields all have Input Masks in American formats. These should be deleted, so we can input data in our format.

- **Enter data directly into the table** takes you to the Datasheet View. This is the default option.

- **Enter data into the table using a form the wizard creates for me** – the Wizard will design a simple form that shows one record at a time. You can use the form or datasheet to input, edit and view records.

Basic steps

1 Select **Modify the table design**.

2 Click [Finish].

3 At the **Table Design** window select a field to be modified.

4 Press **[F6]**.

5 Delete the entry in the **Input Mask** row.

6 Press **[F6]**.

❑ Repeat for all fields as needed, then save the edited design and close the Table Design window.

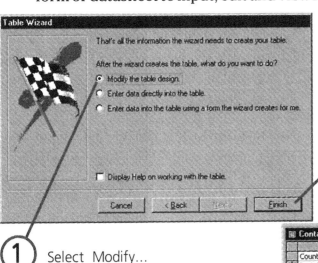

(1) Select Modify...

(2) Click Finish

(3) Select the field

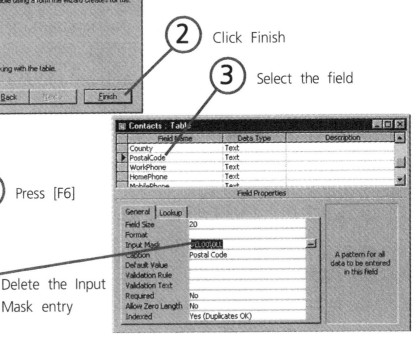

(4) Press [F6]

(5) Delete the Input Mask entry

Basic steps

1 From the Database window, click the **Relationship** tool 🔳.

or

2 Choose **Relationships...** from the **Edit** menu

❑ The **Relationships** and **Show Table** dialog boxes open.

3 If the **Show Table** dialog box doesn't open, click the **Show Table** tool 🔳.

4 Pick the *Accommodation* table from the list.

5 Click [Add] to add it to the **Relationships** window. Add the other tables in the same way if necessary.

6 Click [Close] on the Show Table dialog box.

Relationships

Now that all the tables have been set up, we can establish the other relationships between the tables.

At this stage we want to set 2 relationships – one between the *Accommodation* and the *Price* tables (they are related through the *Price Range* field that appears in both) and another between the *Accommodation* and *Type of Accommodation* tables (related through the *AccCode* field)

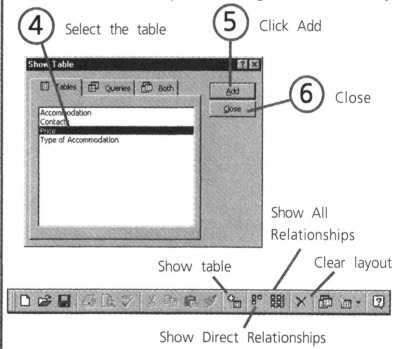

④ Select the table

⑤ Click Add

⑥ Close

Show All Relationships

Show table

Clear layout

Show Direct Relationships

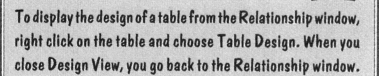

Take note

To display the design of a table from the Relationship window, right click on the table and choose **Table Design**. When you close **Design View**, you go back to the Relationship window.

Tip

Use the tools in the Relationship toolbar to view, edit and save the relationships you set up.

Making and breaking the relationships

We must now indicate how the tables are related. A relationship will normally be between the primary key field in one table and a similar field in another table. In our example the primary key of the *Price* table is related to the *Price Range* field in the *Accommodation* table.

(1) Display the fields

(2) Drag and drop to join

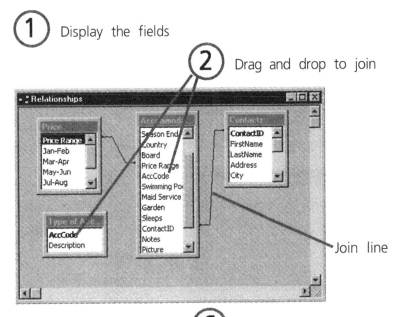

Join line

(6) Create the join

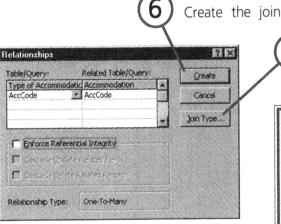

(3) Click to check or edit relationship

1 In the Relationships window, scroll through the list for each table until you can see the fields that are to be related – e.g. *AccCode*.

2 Drag and drop the field name from one table onto the related field in the other table.

3 At the **Relationships** dialog box, if you want to edit the relationship, click [Join Type...].

4 At the **Join Properties** dialog box, choose the type of join required – in our case the first.

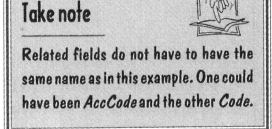

Take note

Related fields do not have to have the same name as in this example. One could have been *AccCode* and the other *Code*.

60

5 Click .

6 At the **Relationships** dialog box, click [Create] to set the relationship. Now, in the **Relationships** window, a line shows the related fields in your tables.

7 If you want to delete a relationship, select the line and press **[Delete]**.

8 Click [Yes] to confirm at the **Delete relationship** prompt.

❑ Ensure that all your tables are related as required.

9 Save the relationships – click 🖫 and close the Relationships window.

You are returned to the Database window.

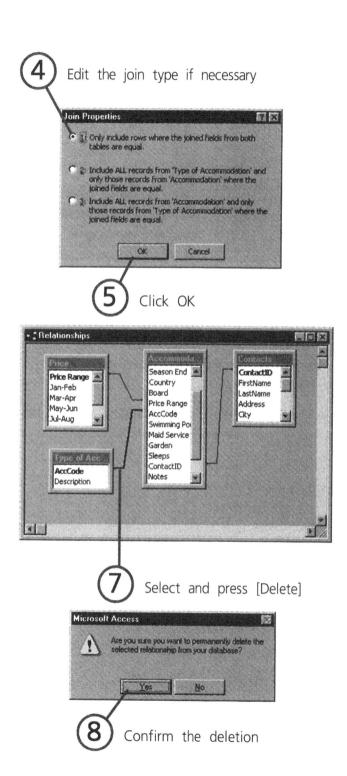

④ Edit the join type if necessary

⑤ Click OK

⑦ Select and press [Delete]

⑧ Confirm the deletion

61

Summary

❑ You must **open the database** to work on it, if it is not already open.

❑ **Table Wizards** can help automate the table design process.

❑ **Check out the Relationships** set by the Table Wizard and edit if necessary.

❑ When using Table Wizard, choose the **Modify table design** option at the chequered flag and locate and delete any Input Masks following the American format.

❑ Most tables within your database will be related to at least one other table.

❑ A **relationship** normally exists between the **primary key field** in one table and a similar field in another.

❑ You can check, make and delete the Relationships betweeb tables in **the Relationships window.**

6   Data entry and edit

Using Datasheet View

Opening a table

Once you have set up the structure of your table and set the relationships, the next stage is data entry. The table must be open for this and it should be displayed in **Datasheet** View (rather than Design View). In this view, each column of the table is a field and each row is a record. Start with the *Type of Accommodation* table, then complete the other three.

Entering data

Type the data required into each field.

Move from field to field in your table using:

[Tab]   to take you forward to the next field;

[Shift]-[Tab]   to take your back to the previous field.

Each record is saved when you move onto the next.

Records in the *Type of Accomodation* table

Current record

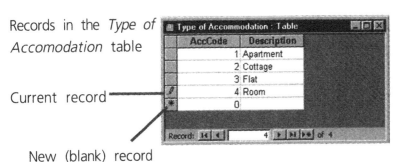

New (blank) record

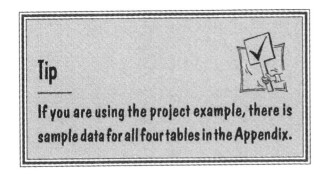

❑ To open a table in Datasheet View

1 Select the **Tables** tab in the **Database** window.

2 Select the table you want to open.

3 Click [**Open**] or double click on the table name.

Take note

If you are working in Design View on a table, you can go directly to Datasheet View by clicking the View tool on the toolbar.

The *Reference* value is
created by AutoNumber

Input Mask   Lookup field   Default value

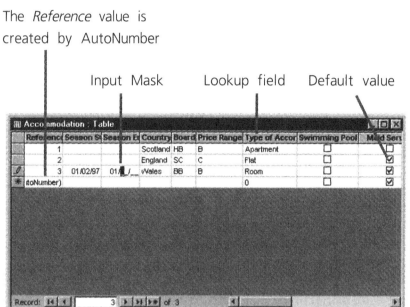

Take note

When entering data,
should you find an error
has been made at the
Design stage, you can go
into Design View to edit
the table design by
clicking

Inappropriate entries

If you enter incompatible data for the data type specified
in a field (e.g. if you put text in a number field, or try to key
something in that disagrees with the Input Mask for that
field), Access will display an error message. This will
either be a standard error message, or one you keyed in
to the Validation Text field at the design stage (page 44).

Take note

Your entries in the *ContactID* field
in the *Accommodation* table need to
correspond to *ContactIDs* in the
Contacts table.

Validation Text message

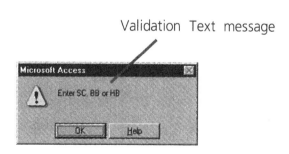

65

Moving around your datasheet

In addition to using [**Tab**] and [**Shift**]-[**Tab**] to move between fields, there are other ways to move around.

● Point and click with the mouse to go to any field (using the vertical and/or horizontal scroll bars as necessary to bring the field into view).

● Use the arrows to the left of the horizontal scroll bar.

● To go to a specific record number, press [**F5**], key in the record number and press [**Enter**].

Editing

You can edit data at any time. If you move onto a field using [**Tab**] or [**Shift**]-[**Tab**] the data in that field is selected.

You can then:

● **Replace the current contents** - just type in the new data while the old is highlighted.

● **Edit the data** – press [**F2**] to deselect the text, then position the insertion point within the field using the [**Arrow**] keys.

● Erase the contents, by pressing [**Delete**].

Take note

If you are working through the project, enter the data into the *Type of Accommodation* table **before** you enter the data into the *Accommodation* table. The *Accommodation* table will lookup the *Type of Accommodation* table for the data held within it.

Basic steps

1 Tab along to the *Type of Accommodation* field.

2 Click the drop-down arrow to display the list of options.

3 Select the one required.

The Lookup field

Notice the *Type of Accommodation* lookup field in the *Accommodation* table – it is a combo box, where you drop down the list of alternatives and select the one required.

(1) Move to the field

(2) Click the drop-down arrow

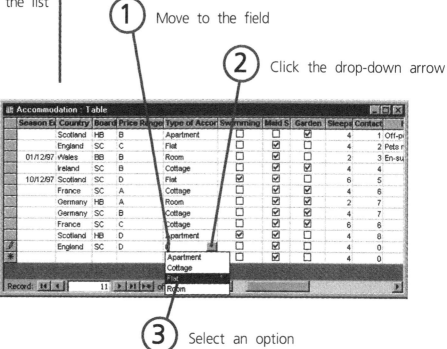

(3) Select an option

Take note

We could have specified the Lookup data type for some of the other fields in our *Accommodation* table e.g. *Board, Price Range, Contact* and *Country*. It is a useful data type for fields that have a limited number of possible input options.

Pictures as OLE Objects

If you wish to insert a picture in the OLE Object field in the *Accommodation* table you can use some of the pictures in the Clip Gallery to practice with.

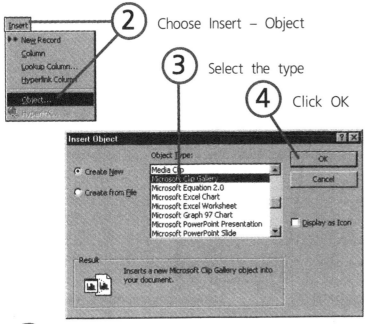

Choose Insert – Object

Select the type

Click OK

1 Tab along to the Picture field.

2 Choose **Object** from the **Insert** menu.

3 Select the **Object Type** – in this example **Microsoft Clip Gallery**.

4 Click OK.

5 Select the tab required – **Clip Art**.

6 Choose a picture.

7 Click Insert.

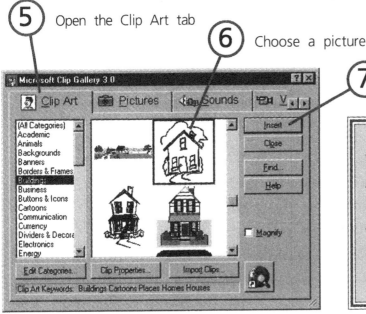

Open the Clip Art tab

Choose a picture

Click Insert

Take note

In Datasheet View Access displays the name of the object, e.g. Microsoft Clip Gallery, not the actual image.

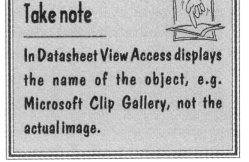

Basic steps

1 Tab along to the Hyperlink field.

2 Click the **Insert Hyperlink** tool 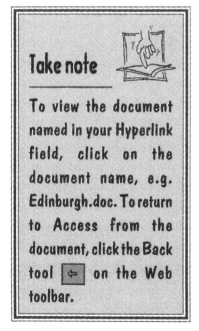.

3 Enter the path to your document.

Or

4 Click ![Browse...] and locate the document required.

5 Click ![OK].

Take note

To view the document named in your Hyperlink field, click on the document name, e.g. Edinburgh.doc. To return to Access from the document, click the Back tool ⇦ on the Web toolbar.

Hyperlinks to documents

General information about the areas in which the properties are located could be held in a set of Word documents – use any Word document to try this out.

These documents can be linked to the table through a Hyperlink in the Hyperlink field we set up.

③ Enter the path

④ Browse for the file

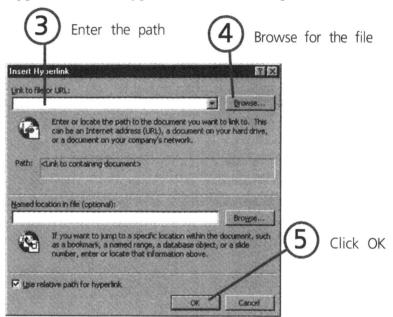

⑤ Click OK

The source, not the picture, is displayed in Datasheet View

Hyperlink to Word document

69

Adding and deleting records

Adding new records

When adding new records to your table, you add them to the end of the list of existing records. If you do not really want them at the end of the list, you will soon find out that it is very easy to sort the records into the order you want (rather than leaving them in input order).

1 Click the **New Record** tool ▶* or button ▶*.

2 You are moved to the first field of the first empty row under the existing records.

3 Key in the new record(s).

4 Close the datasheet or continue editing as required.

④ Close?

Reference	Season St	Season Er	Country	Board	Price Range	Type of Accor	Swimming	Maid S
8			Germany	SC	B	Cottage	☐	☑
9			France	SC	C	Cottage	☐	☑
10			Scotland	HB	D	Apartment	☑	☑
11			England	SC	D	Flat	☑	☑
12			Wales	BB	E	Apartment	☑	☐
13			Scotland	SC	E	Flat	☐	☑
14			Italy	SC	C	Cottage	☑	☑
15			Spain	SC	D	Apartment	☑	☑
16			England	SC	C	Cottage	☐	☑
17			France	BB	C	Room	☐	☑
18			Orkney	SC	B	Cottage	☐	☑
19			Jersey	SC	C	Apartment	☑	☑
20			Ireland	HB	D	Room	☑	☑
* (toNumber)						0	☐	☑

Record: ◄◄ ◄ 13 ► ►◄ ►* of 20

③ Enter detail

② New record row

① Click New Record

Keyboard shortcuts

[PageUp]	Up a page
[↑]	Current field, previous record
[PageDn]	Down a page
[↓]	Current field, next record
[Home]	First field, current record
[End]	Last field, current record

[Ctrl]-[PageUp]	Left a page
[Ctrl]-[↑]	Current field, first record
[Ctrl]-[PageDn]	Right a page
[Ctrl]-[↓]	Current field, last record
[Ctrl]-[Home]	First field, first record
[Ctrl]-[End]	Last field, last record

Basic steps

1 Click in the row selector area to select the record you no longer require.

2 Press **[Delete]** or click the Delete record tool .

3 At the **Delete record** prompt click [Yes] if you are sure. The record is then deleted.

Take note

To select several adjacent records, click and drag in the row selector area until you have highlighted all the records you want to delete.

Deleting records

When some of your records become redundant, you will want to delete them. Be careful when deleting records — make sure you are really finished with them first!

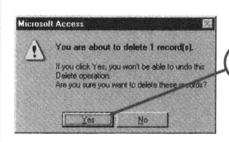

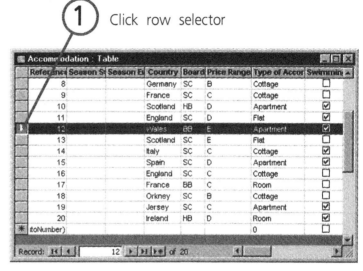

① Click row selector

② Press [Delete]

③ Confirm deletion

Using Form View

As an altern working in Datasheet view you could let Access create a basic form for you using AutoForm.

AutoForm will take the fields, and arrange them in a simple list layout that displays one record at a time. (If there are lots of fields in each record you may have to scroll through the form to view them all.) The table name will be displayed at the top of each record.

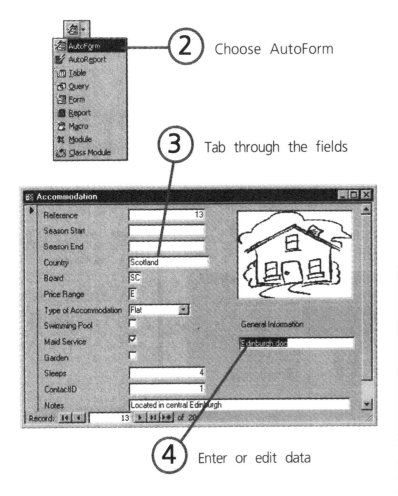

② Choose AutoForm

③ Tab through the fields

④ Enter or edit data

1 At the **Database** window select the table.

2 Pick **AutoForm** from the **New Object** list.

❑ A simple form is displayed on the screen

3 Use [Tab] or [Shift]-[Tab] to move between fields (or point and click with the mouse).

4 At each field, key in the required data.

5 When you reach the last field, pressing [Tab] takes you to the first field in the next record.

Take note

In the illustration, the OLE Object field and Hyperlink field have been moved so that you can see the complete form on the screen at the one time. You will learn how to do this on page 115.

Basic steps

1 Click the **Save** tool .

or

2 If you have closed the form without saving, click [Yes] at the **Save changes** prompt.

3 At the **Save As** dialog box enter a name e.g. *Accommodation Simple Form.*

4 Click [OK].

❑ The form will be listed on the **Forms** tab of the Database window.

Take note

When you enter data through a form, the data is recorded in the associated table. If you opt not to save the form, the data is still saved.

Naming your form

When you have keyed in all the data, you will want to return to your Database window.

Save and name the form before you go. You will be prompted to do this if you try to close without saving.

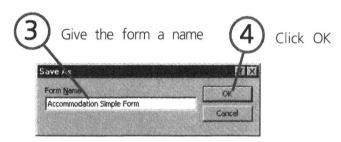

③ Give the form a name   ④ Click OK

The Form is listed in the Database window

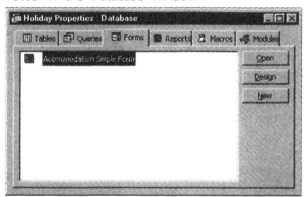

Tip

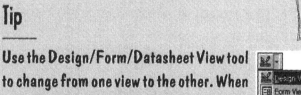

Use the Design/Form/Datasheet View tool to change from one view to the other. When entering data, you can switch freely between Form and Datasheet Views. The data will all be saved in the same table.

See Chapter 10 for more information on form design.

Summary

- To **open a table** in **Datasheet view**, select the Tables tab on the Database window, then double click the table name.

- If the data you enter violates a **Validation rule**, an error mesage is displayed.

- To **move between fields** in your datasheet use **[Tab]** or **[Shift]-[Tab]**, the mouse or the keyboard shortcuts.

- To **move between records** use the arrows on the left of the status bar, or the scroll bars and the mouse, or the keyboard shortcuts.

- To **go to a specific record** press **[F5]**, key in the record number and press [Enter].

- The **contents of a field** can be edited, replaced or deleted during initial data entry or at any later time.

- The values in a **Lookup field** are displayed in a drop-down list.

- To complete an **OLE Object field**, choose Object... from the Insert menu and locate the object required.

- **Hyperlink fields** can contain a path to a file or an Internet address.

- To display your **records in a form layout**, click the **Autoform** tool on the toolbar.

- To **change your view** use the **View** tool on the toolbar.

- To **add a record** to your table, click the New Record tool on the toolbar, then key in the detail.

- To **delete a record**, select it, then press **[Delete]**.

Take note

If you are working through the project in this book, add the data in the Appendix to all four tables before continuing.

7 Redesigning a table

Adding a field

New fields can easily be added to an existing table. Try adding two fields to the *Accommodation* table.

- *Town* has the Text data type, and will fit above *Country*;

- *Star Rating* will go above *ContactID*. This field should have the Number data type and an Integer format. Add a Validation Rule set to accept only a 1 or 2 or 3 or 4 (our star rating system).

- If you are working through the project make up some *Town* and *Star Rating* details.

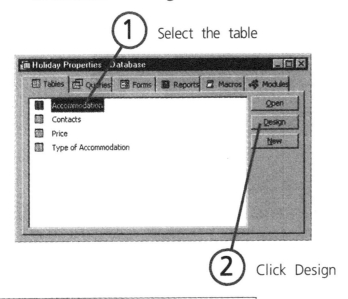

① Select the table

② Click Design

Take note

To add a field at the end of your field list, simply scroll down to the first empty row, and key in the details required.

1 At the **Database** window, select the Table whose design you want to edit.

2 Click **Design**.

3 Select the row (field) that you want to have below the new one.

4 Click the Insert Rows tool. A new field is added *above* the selected one.

5 Define the field name, data type, description, and field properties.

6 Add other fields as required.

7 Save the changes – click the Save tool.

8 Respond to the **Data Integrity Rules** prompt.

9 Close the Design window by clicking its Close button.

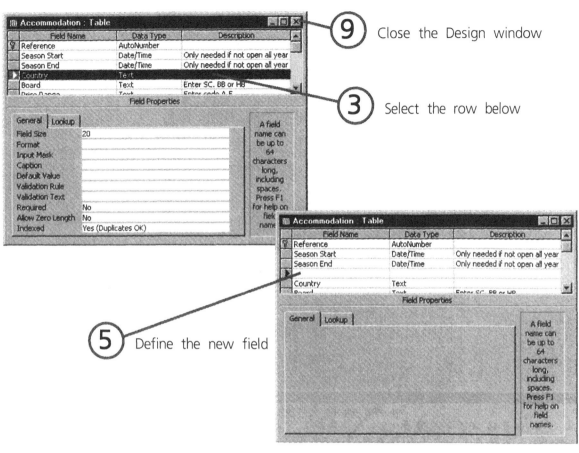

⑨ Close the Design window

③ Select the row below

⑤ Define the new field

Take note

If you add Validation Rules (see page 41) to a new field, this prompt appears when you try to save the new design.

With a new field, which contains no data, click [No].
If you have changed the properties of an existing field (with data in it) click [Yes] to check the data against the new rules or [No] to leave it unchecked.

Microsoft Access

⚠ Data integrity rules have been changed; existing data may not be valid for the new rules.

This process may take a long time. Do you want the existing data to be tested with the new rules?

[Yes]   [No]   [Cancel]

Deleting a field

Redundant fields are just as easily removed. Any data held within a field that you delete is permanently erased – so be careful with this one!

● Before deleting a field, go into Datasheet View. If the field contains information in any record, think carefully and be sure it is okay to delete.

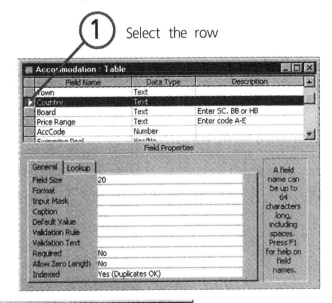

Select the row

Confirm the deletion

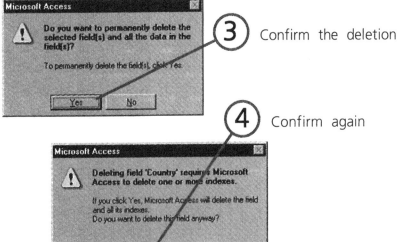

Confirm again

1 Select the row (field) you want to delete.

2 Click the **Delete Rows** tool .

3 Confirm the deletion at the prompt.

4 If an **Index** will also be deleted, you will be prompted to confirm the deletion again.

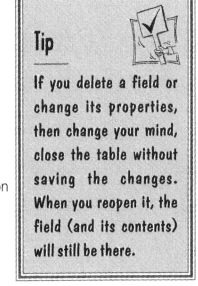

Tip

If you delete a field or change its properties, then change your mind, close the table without saving the changes. When you reopen it, the field (and its contents) will still be there.

Basic steps

1 Select a **Currency** field.

2 Press **[F6]** to move to the lower pane.

3 Open the **Decimal Places** list and change the property to 0.

4 Repeat for all fields.

❑ **Moving fields**

5 In Design View, click in the selector bar.

6 With the pointer in the selector bar area, drag and drop the field into its new position.

7 Save the changes and close the window.

Take note

In Datasheet View, you can move a field by dragging the field name at the top of the column.

Field properties can also be modified as required. In the *Price* table, we can change the field properties of the fields with a **Currency** data type to show 0 decimal places.

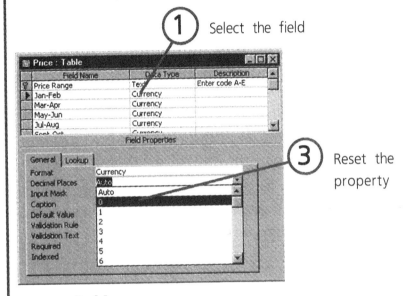

① Select the field

③ Reset the property

Moving fields

You can change the order of your fields in either Design or Datasheet View.

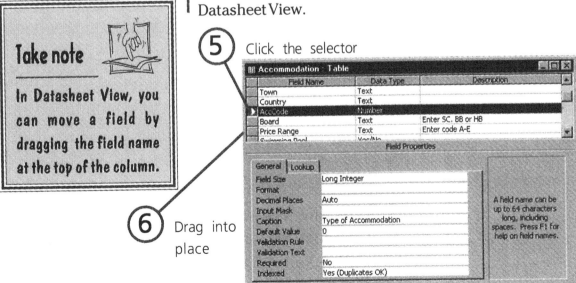

⑤ Click the selector

⑥ Drag into place

Primary key and indexes

You may decide that the field that you originally set as your Primary Key is no longer appropriate.

- Changing the primary key is simply a case of setting a new one (see page 29);

- Removing the primary key without setting a new one is also very easy. The primary key tool is a toggle – it switches the status on and off. Select the field that currently has primary key status and click the Primary Key tool. (Set your primary key again if necessary.)

You can display a list of the fields that you have indexed in your table. This gives you a quick check on what has and hasn't been indexed.

1 In Design View, click the **Indexes** tool .

2 A list of the indexed fields is displayed.

3 Click the **Indexes** tool again to close the dialog box (or click its **Close** button).

③ Close when done

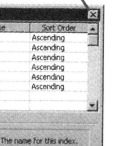

② List of indexed fields

Take note

You must be in **Design View** to view your indexes.

Take note

Viewing the Indexes dialog box can be useful to let you check what fields have and have not been indexed — it's a lot quicker then checking each field individually in Design View.

Basic steps

1 Open the *Accommodation* table in Design View.

2 Move the insertion point to the *Town* field.

3 Press [F6] to go to the lower pane.

4 Set the *Indexed* field to *Yes (Duplicates OK)*.

5 Do the same with the *Star Rating* field.

6 Save the changes.

7 Close the table.

Tip

To see a list of the Indexed fields in your table, open the Indexes dialog box - click the Indexes tool. You can edit the properties of any index entry — ie Index Name, Sort Order, Primary key status etc — from this dialog box.

Adjusting indexes

Fields can be indexed at the initial design stage, or during a later edit of the design.

You should index those fields you will want to sort on or search on, as it speeds up sorting and searching.

In the *Accommodation* table, we could index the *Town* and *Star Rating* fields, so we could to sort accommodation into town order, or search for accommodation in certain towns or with specific star ratings.

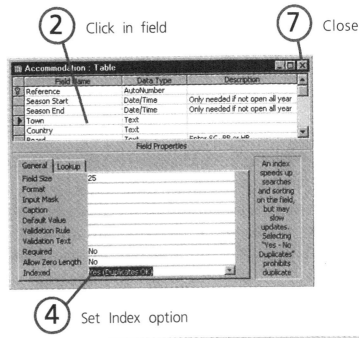

Set Index option

New list of indexed fields

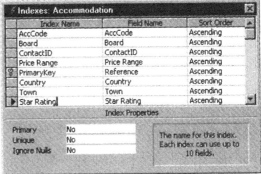

Summary

- To **add a field in the middle** of your table, select the field that will be below your new field and click the Insert Rows tool on the Toolbar.

- To **add a field to the end** of your field list, scroll down to the end of the list and key in the new field details.

- To **delete a field**, select the row, make sure that it is the right one and you really don't want it, then click the Delete Rows tool on the toolbar.

- **Field Properties** are easily changed – select the field whose properties are to be changed, press [F6] to move to the lower pane, make the changes, then press [F6] to return to the upper pane.

- The **order or fields** can be rearranged in either Design or Datasheet View.

- To **change the primary key**, simply set a new one as required.

- To **remove the primary key status** from a field, and not set another field as the primary key, select the current primary key field, then click the primary key tool to switch the status off.

- Fields that are likely to be **sorted** or **searched** on should be indexed.

- Remember to **save** your edited Design.

8 Datasheet display

Gridlines

So far, we have been content with the way our tables appear on the screen. However, depending on the number of fields in your table, and what you want to look at, you may need to change the format of your datasheet.

You can also print data from your table in Datasheet View, so you might want to consider customising the datasheet format before you print (see page 93).

By default, the gridlines are displayed between the rows and columns of your table. Most of the time this is what you want, but, particularly if you are going to print your table in Datasheet View, you might prefer to switch them off. Viewing and hiding gridlines is an on/off toggle – you switch them on and off using the same command sequence.

It is assumed the gridlines are displayed at this stage.

(see page 93)

Basic steps

1 Open the **Format** menu.

2 Click **Cells...**

3 Complete the **Cells Effects** dialog box as required.

4 Click [OK].

Take note

If you make the Gridline colour the same as the background colour, your gridlines are 'hidden'.

---

1. Open the Format menu

2. Select Cells...

3. Set the options

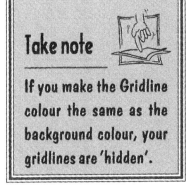

4. Click OK

Check the effect in the Sample box

Basic steps

1 Select one column by clicking in the Field Name row.

or

Select a set of adjacent columns by dragging along the field name row.

2 Choose **Hide Columns** from the **Format** menu.

You may not want all the columns in your table to be visible. You may be concentrating on a task that only uses certain fields and decide to hide the ones that are of no concern at the moment, or you might want to print out only certain columns from your datasheet.

① Select the column(s)

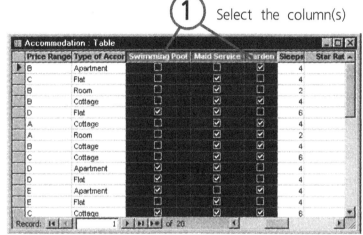

② Use Format – Hide Columns

Columns hidden

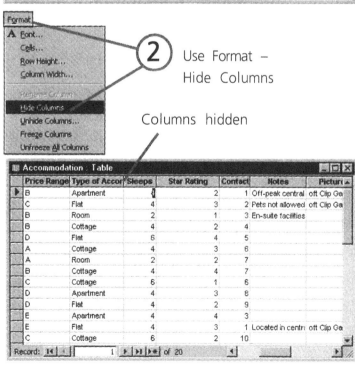

Take note

You can also hide columns by dragging the vertical line between the field names left, until the field to the left of the line disappears. Columns that appear hidden this way may register 'showing' in the Show Columns dialog box. You must hide the column completely to give it 'hidden' status.

Showing columns

If you have hidden some columns, there will come a time when you need to show them again. The easiest way to reveal hidden columns is to use the Unhide Columns command in the Format menu.

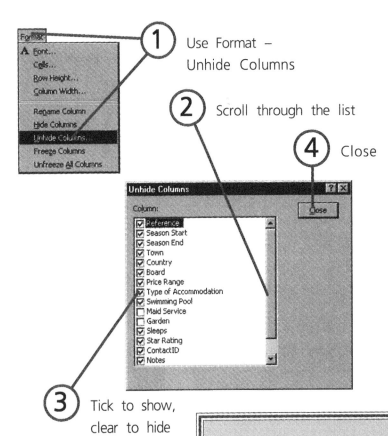

Use Format –
Unhide Columns

Scroll through the list

Close

Tick to show,
clear to hide

Basic steps

1 Open the **Format** menu and choose **Unhide Columns**.

❑ The **Unhide columns** dialog box appears. The columns currently showing have a tick beside them.

2 Scroll up and down the list to locate the field name you want if necessary.

3 Toggle the **Show/Hide** status by selecting the fields you wish to show, or deselecting those you wish to hide.

4 When you have specified what fields to show, and which to hide, click [Close].

Take note

You can 'show' hidden columns using the click and drag method, but it can be tricky! Locating the column border in the field name row (where one border overlays another when columns are hidden) can be a frustrating exercise using the mouse!

Basic steps

1 Choose **Font...** from the **Format** menu.

2 In the **Font** dialog box, select the font, size and style.

· The **Sample** area shows the effect your selections will have on the characters.

3 Click [OK] to return to the datasheet with your new settings.

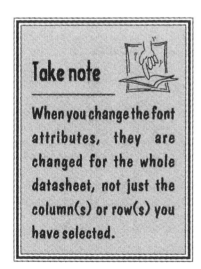

Take note

When you change the font attributes, they are changed for the whole datasheet, not just the column(s) or row(s) you have selected.

The default character style (font) is Arial, 10 point. You may want to change the font style or size if you are formatting your datasheet with a view to printing it. You might want to use a larger font, or make the print bold for example.

You can change the font style and/or size by using the **Font** dialog box.

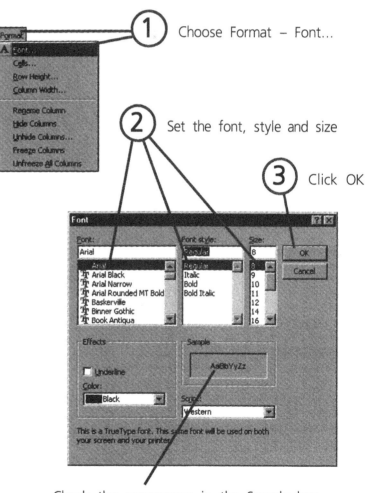

① Choose Format – Font...

② Set the font, style and size

③ Click OK

Check the appearance in the Sample box

Widths and heights

The **column widths** are initially determined by the field size or the field name size that appears at the top of each column. You can change the displayed width when in Datasheet View. Width is measured in characters.

You can change the **row height** for all the records in your datasheet. You may wish to do this if you want to see more records on your screen at one time. Height is measured in **points**, the same as font sizes.

Basic steps

- Setting Column Width
1 Select the column(s).
2 Choose **Column Width** from the **Format** menu.
3 Set the required width, or select the Standard Width box.
4 Click [OK].
- Setting Row Height
5 Choose **Row Height** from the **Format** menu.
6 Set the height, or select the Standard Height box.
7 Click [OK].

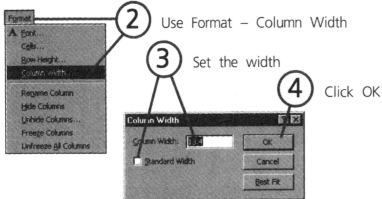

Use Format – Column Width

Set the width

Click OK

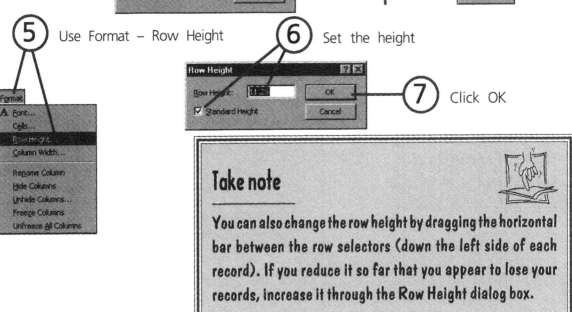

Use Format – Row Height

Set the height

Click OK

Take note

You can also change the row height by dragging the horizontal bar between the row selectors (down the left side of each record). If you reduce it so far that you appear to lose your records, increase it through the Row Height dialog box.

Freezing columns

1 Select the column(s).

2 Choose **Freeze Columns** from the **Format** menu.

3 The column(s) are moved, if necessary, and frozen at the left of the table.

❑ **To unfreeze columns**

4 Choose **Unfreeze All Columns** from the **Format** menu.

There will be times that you need to view columns, which are distant from each other in your table, on the screen at the same time. This can be done by hiding (see page 85) or by **freezing** columns at the left side of your table. They will remain in position while the other columns can be scrolled in and out of sight. If gridlines are not displayed, a thick line appears to the right of the frozen columns.

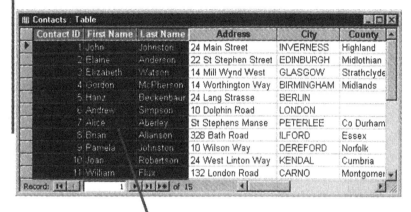

(1) Select the column(s)

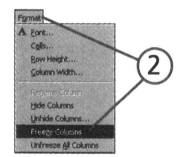

(2) Use Format – Freeze Columns

(3) Columns frozen

Take note

Columns that have been frozen, remain at the left edge when unfrozen.

The thick line marks the edge of the frozen columns

Print Preview

Now that you have some data in your table(s), you will most likely want to print it out at some stage. There are various ways of doing this, but an easy way to begin with is to print from Datasheet View.

Once the datasheet display has been formatted to your satisfaction, you can print the table.

Do a Print Preview first and check that the layout is okay on screen, before you commit it to paper.

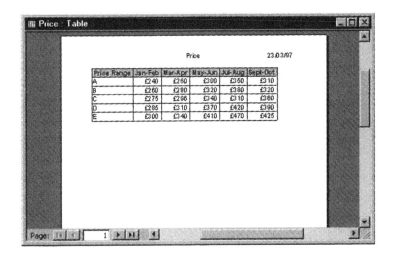

Print Preview toolbar

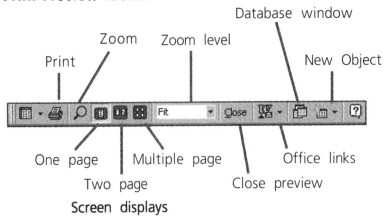

 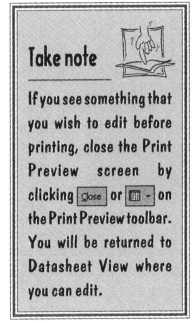
Take note

If you see something that you wish to edit before printing, close the Print Preview screen by clicking [Close] or [▦ ▾] on the Print Preview toolbar. You will be returned to Datasheet View where you can edit.

90

Basic steps

Zoom

1 Move your mouse pointer (it should look like a magnifying glass) over the area of the table you want to zoom in on.

2 Click the left mouse button.

3 You are zoomed in, so you can read the data.

4 Use the scroll bars to bring other areas of the table into view.

5 Click the left mouse button again to zoom out.

❑ The Zoom tool on the Print Preview toolbar acts as a zoom in/zoom out toggle too.

In Print Preview, it is very difficult (if not impossible) to read the data being displayed. This is not usually a problem, as you are really just checking the presentation of the data, not the detail. However, if you want to check an entry, you can zoom in to get a better look!

You cannot edit the data from the Print Preview screen – if you notice something is inaccurate or you want to change the formatting of the table, you must close Print Preview and return to the datasheet to make the changes.

③ Zoomed in on the table

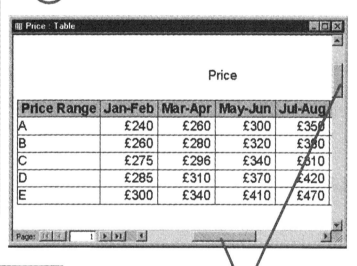

④ Scroll to see other parts

Tip

The mouse click and the 🔍 tool toggle between close up and full page. For better control of the magnification, use the Zoom level drop-down list.

Page Setup

If you need to change the margins or orientation of your page, use the Page Setup dialog box to make the necessary changes. You can move to the Page Setup dialog box from the Print Preview screen or from Datasheet View.

1 Open the **File** menu.

2 Select **Page Setup**.

3 Complete the **Page Setup** dialog box as required.

4 Click OK .

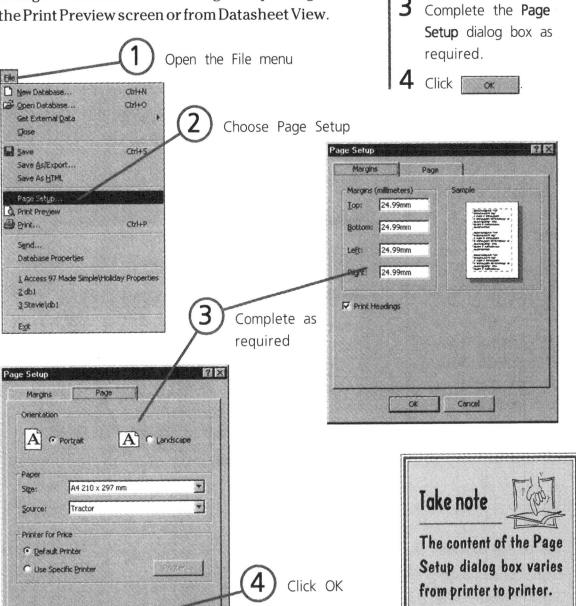

Open the File menu

Choose Page Setup

Complete as required

Click OK

Take note

The content of the Page Setup dialog box varies from printer to printer.

92

Basic steps

1 If you want to print certain records, select them now.

2 Choose **Print** from the **File** menu.

3 Complete the **Print** dialog box as required.

4 Click [OK].

If the table is formatted and the Page Setup is okay, you can go ahead and print your table. You can print directly from Datasheet View, or from the Print Preview screen. It does not matter whether you are in Datasheet Vview or the Print Preview screen, the routine is the same.

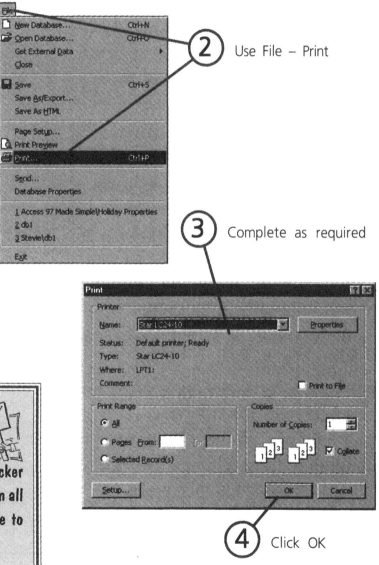

② Use File – Print

③ Complete as required

④ Click OK

Take note

To send your table directly to the printer, using the default print settings, click the Print tool 🖨.

Tip

Multiple copies are printed quicker uncollated – i.e. all page 1s then all page 2s, etc, but you will have to collate them by hand later.

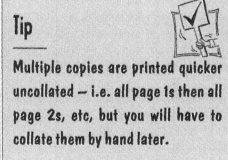

Summary

- The **Gridlines** can be changed from the Cells Effects dialog box.

- To **hide columns**, select the columns you want to hide then choose Format – Hide Columns.

- To **show hidden columns**, choose Format – Unhide Columns and complete the dialog box as required.

- To change **the font** used in your datasheet, choose Format – Font and select from the options.

- To change the **width of columns** choose Format – Column Width, and set the width in the dialog box.

- To customise the **row height**, choose Format – Row Height and specify the required height.

- To **stop columns scrolling off the screen**, select them and choose Format – Freeze Columns.

- To **unfreeze your columns**, choose Format – Unfreeze All Columns.

- To **preview** your datasheet before printing, click the Print Preview tool on the toolbar.

- To check **details on the Print Preview** screen, zoom in and out as required.

- To change the **margins**, **paper size** or **orientation** of the paper, go into Page Setup.

- To **print your datasheet**, click the Print tool on the Datasheet toolbar or on the Print Preview toolbar.

9 Sorting and searching

Find

With larger databases, it is impractical to locate records by scrolling through, reading each row. Instead, you can use the **Find** command, which will locate records that contain a specified item of text. Find works most efficiently if you know what field the data is in (so you don't need to search the whole table), and the field is *indexed*.

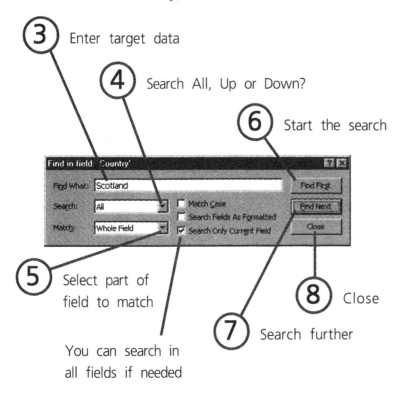

③ Enter target data

④ Search All, Up or Down?

⑥ Start the search

⑤ Select part of field to match

⑧ Close

⑦ Search further

You can search in all fields if needed

Tip

When the **Find** dialog box appears, drag on its title bar to move it so that it does not obscure the data you are working with.

Basic steps

1 If you know what field the data is in, position the insertion point in the field column in Datasheet View before you start.

2 Click the **Find** tool .

3 Key the target data in the **Find What:** area.

4 In **Search:** specify whether to search the whole table, or up or down from the current record.

5 In **Match:** indicate where the data appears in the field.

6 Click [Find First] to start the search.

7 Click [Find Next] after you have found one and want the next match.

8 Click [Close] when you have found what you want.

Basic steps

1 Select the text you want to base your filter on, e.g. 'Scotland' in the *Country* field.

2 Click the **Filter By Selection** tool.

❑ Records matching the selection are displayed.

3 Repeat the process if you want a sub-set of your new list, e.g. only self-catering properties.

4 Click the **Remove Filter** tool to display all your records again.

Filter By Selection

When working within a table, you might want to display a subset of the records held based on some criteria, e.g. all the properties in Scotland. You can use **Filter By Selection** techniques for this.

① Select the criteria

Ref	Season Start	Season End	Town	Country	Board	Price	Type of Accomm
1			Aberdeen	Scotland	HB	B	Apartment
2			Slough	England	SC	C	Flat
3	01/02/97	01/12/97	Cardiff	Wales	BB	B	Room
4			Cork	Ireland	SC	B	Cottage
5	18/01/97	10/12/97	Inverness	Scotland	SC	D	Flat
6			Paris	France	SC	A	Cottage
7			Berlin	Germany	HB	A	Room
8			Dusseldorf	Germany	SC	B	Cottage
9			Paris	France	SC	C	Cottage

Record: 1 of 20

Display after first level of filtering

Ref	Season Start	Season End	Town	Country	Board	Price	Type of Accommoda
1			Aberdeen	Scotland	HB	B	Apartment
5	18/01/97	10/12/97	Inverness	Scotland	SC	D	Flat
10			Edinburgh	Scotland	HB	D	Apartment
13			Elie	Scotland	SC	E	Flat
(er)						0	

Record: 1 of 4 (Filtered)

③ Select again?

Take note

You can repeat the filter process as many times as you like, to get down to the records you want.

Filter By Form

As an alternative to using Filter By Selection, you could use Filter By Form. Using Filter By Form, you can specify multiple criteria at the same time, rather than one at a time, e.g. 'England' in *Country* and 'SC' in *Board*.

You can also set alternative criteria, using the **Or** tab. If 'Scotland' in *Country* was selected here, the filter would pick up properties in either country.

1 Click the **Filter By Form** tool .

❏ As you move from field to field, you will notice that each becomes a Combo type box, with a drop-down arrow.

2 Select the criteria required from the drop-down lists.

3 Switch to the **Or** tab and set options here if alternatives are wanted.

4 Click the **Apply Filter** tool.

② Set criteria

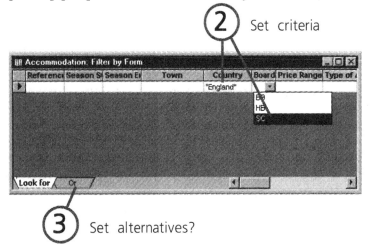

③ Set alternatives?

Self-catering in England

Self-catering in England
or
Self-catering in Scotland

Basic steps

1 Open the table you want to sort (in our case *Accommodation*).

2 Put the insertion point anywhere in the field you want to sort your records on.

3 Click the 🔼 or 🔽 tool.

❑ The records are sorted in Ascending or Descending order, as selected.

Take note

You can be anywhere, in any row, in the field you want to sort on. The whole table will be sorted in ascending or descending order on the data in that field.

When you key records into your table, they appear in the order they were input, or that of the primary key if one is set. There will be times when you need the records in a different order, ascending or descending, using some other field in the table. For example, in the *Accommodation* table, you might decide to rearrange, or **sort**, your records into *Country*, *Town* or *Star Rating* order.

Sorting your records on one field is very easy. We could use the *Accommodation* table to try this out.

① Open the table

② Click in the field you wish to sort on

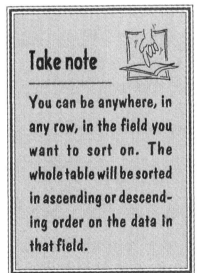

Saving queries

If you have set up a complex set of criteria in the **Advanced Filter/Sort** grid (see page 100), you might want to save it, so you can use it again. Click the **Save As Query** tool 💾 on the **Advanced Filter/Sort** toolbar and enter a meaningful name at the Save As dialog box. The criteria are saved as a **Query**.

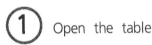

Multi-level sorts

If you need to sort your table on more than one field, you have to set the sort up as a **Query**. You can do this by going into the **Advanced Filter/Sort** dialog box.

Multi-level sorts take longer than single field sorts, and obviously the more levels you sort to, the longer it takes.

We'll do a simple multi-level sort, rearranging the records in the *Accommodation* table by *Country*, then by *Town*.

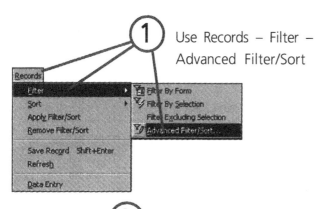

① Use Records – Filter – Advanced Filter/Sort

② Double click each sorting field

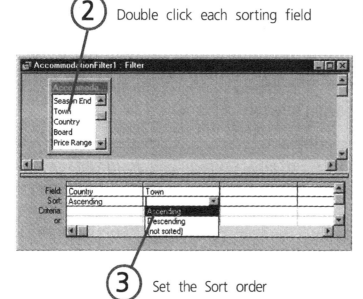

③ Set the Sort order

1 Choose **Filter**, then **Advanced Filter/Sort...** from the **Records** menu.

2 Double click on each field required in the table list to add it to the grid in the lower part of the screen.

3 Select Ascending or Descending Sort order for each field from the drop-down list.

4 Click the **Apply/Remove Filter** tool .

5 The sorted table is displayed.

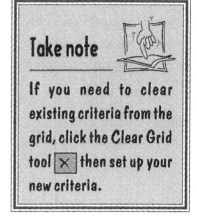

Take note

If you need to clear existing criteria from the grid, click the Clear Grid tool ⊠ then set up your new criteria.

Multi-table queries

Basic steps

❑ **Adding the tables**

1 Select **Query** from the **New Object** list.

or

2 Click [New] on the **Queries** tab.

3 At the **New Query** dialog box, choose **Design View**.

4 Click [OK].

❑ This opens the Select Query and Show Table dialog boxes, where you specify the tables you want to query and set up your criteria.

cont...

If you have more than one table in your database, you may need to interrogate several tables at the same time in order to locate the information you require.

This example draws data from three tables. I want to find properties that sleep more than four people, and for each matching property, I want details of:-

● what town the property is in (*Accommodation*);

● the type of property (*Accommodation*);

● the contact's name and telephone number (*Contacts*);

● the cost of the property in May/June (*Price*).

To do this in Access you set up a query from the Database window.

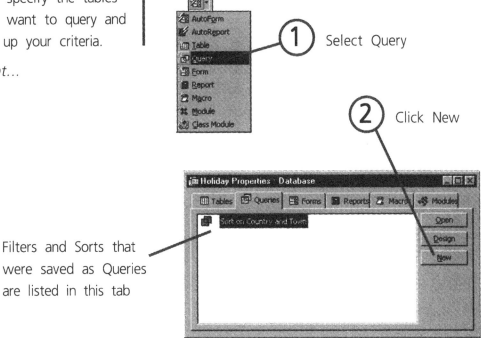

① Select Query

② Click New

Filters and Sorts that were saved as Queries are listed in this tab

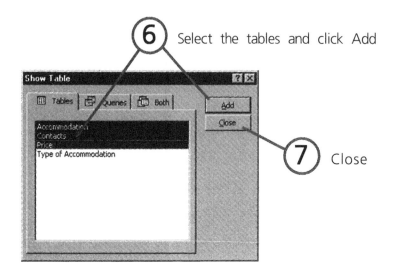

⑥ Select the tables and click Add

⑦ Close

...cont

5 The **Show Table** dialog box should be open. If it is not, click the **Show Table** tool 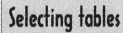.

6 Select the table(s) that you want to query and click Add .

7 When all the necessary tables have been added, click Close to close the dialog box.

Join lines

In the upper half of the **Select Query** dialog box, the join lines between the tables are displayed. These lines indicate the fields that relate one table to another. Here the *Accommodation* and *Contacts* tables are related through the *ContactID* field. The *Accommodation* and *Price* tables are related through the *PriceRange* field. The primary key in each table is displayed in bold type in the field list.

Selecting tables

One table – click on it.

Adjacent tables – click on the first, then hold [Shift] down and click on the last.

Non-adjacent tables – click on the first, then hold [Ctrl] down and click on each of the others.

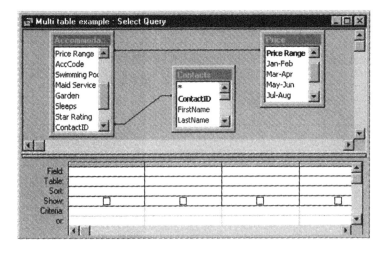

Setting the query criteria

1 Select fields for inclusion by double clicking on them in their table lists.

2 Set the sort and/or selection criteria (if required).

3 If you do not want to display the field contents when you run the query, clear the **Show** checkbox.

4 Click [💾] to save the query.

5 Give the query a suitable name.

6 Click [OK].

cont...

The next stage is to select fields to be included in the output, and to specify any criteria that are to be used to select records.

We want the *Town* and *Sleeps* fields from the *Accommodation* table, with the criteria **>4** (more than 4) set for *Sleeps*; *FirstName*, *LastName* and *HomePhone* from the *Contacts* table and *May-June* from the *Price* table.

If we set **Sort** mode, we can also determine the order of records in the final output.

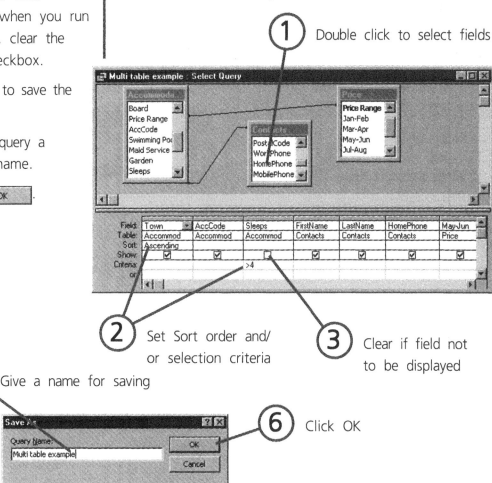

① Double click to select fields

② Set Sort order and/ or selection criteria

③ Clear if field not to be displayed

⑤ Give a name for saving

⑥ Click OK

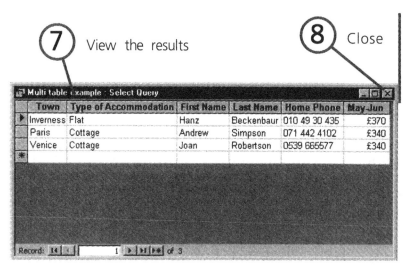

⑦ View the results

⑧ Close

...cont

7 View the results of the query by going into Datasheet View – click the View tool 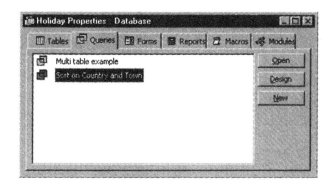.

8 Close the query.

Take note

The query can be found on the Queries tab in the Database window.

Relational operators

When setting criteria you can use relational operators:

> more than   < less than
= equal to   <> not equal to
>= more than or equal to   <= less than or equal to

These are mainly used for Number or Date/Time fields, but can be used with Text.

> "H" means after H in the alphabet.

Basic steps

1 Open the **Database** window.

2 Select the **Queries** tab.

3 Select the query name.

4 Click [Open].

❑ The table is opened, listing the records in the order specified by the sort criteria, or the sub-set of records selected by a filter.

If you have saved a query, you will want to re-run it at some stage. This is easily done from the Database window.

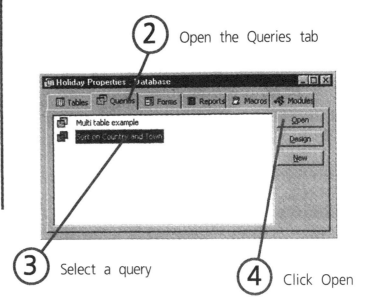

② Open the Queries tab

③ Select a query

④ Click Open

The sorted or filtered table is displayed

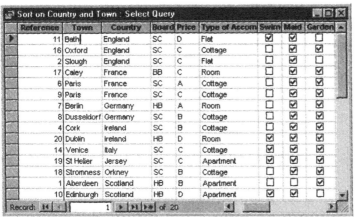

Tip

You can double click the query name on the Queries tab to open the query and run it.

Take note

Remember to save a query if you want to be able to reuse it.

Editing a query

Editing from the Database window is very similar to setting up a new query – you're just not starting from scratch! New criteria may be added, and existing ones removed or changed.

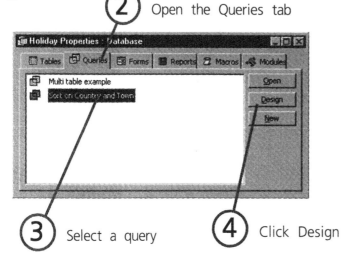

② Open the Queries tab

③ Select a query

④ Click Design

⑤ Check and update

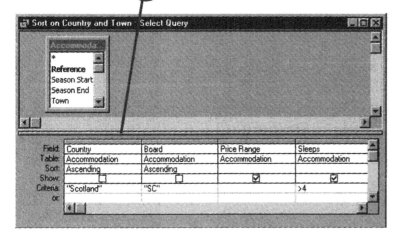

Basic steps

1 Open the **Database** window.

2 Select the **Queries** tab.

3 Select the query name.

4 Click Design .

5 At the **Select Query** dialog box check and update your sort or selection criteria as necessary.

6 Save the query and/or take it into Datasheet View ▦ ▾.

Tip

If you want to edit from the result screen, click the View tool to return to the Select Query screen.

Basic steps

1 Click [**New**] on the Queries tab at the Database window.

or

2 Choose **Query** from the **New Object** list.

3 Choose **Crosstab Query Wizard**.

4 Click [OK].

When we were building up tables, we found there was a Table Wizard to help with the process. There is also a Wizard to take you through the process of building up a query. The Query Wizard, however, provides a useful way of creating rather complex queries – queries that you might find pretty difficult, if not impossible, to do without spending much more time learning Access.

To demonstrate the Query Wizard feature, we will build a query that will interrogate the *Accommodation* table to find out how many properties we have in each country. We then want to break down the total number of properties, so we can tell how many properties each contact has in each country.

To do this, we will use a **Crosstab Query Wizard**. When you run this, you will have to specify:

● the tables or queries to use;
● the field(s) detail you wish to display in each row;
● the field you wish to use for column headings;
● the type of calculation required.

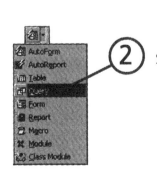

② Select Query

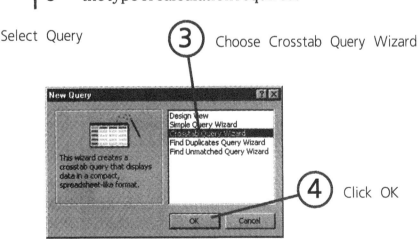

③ Choose Crosstab Query Wizard

④ Click OK

① Select the table

1 Specify the table that contains the detail we want to have in our result table (in our case, *Accommodation*).

2 Specify the field or fields (maximum of 3) you wish to use as row headings (*Country* in this example).

3 Select the field you want to use as column headings (*ContactID*).

4 Specify the calculation required at each row/ column intersection (**Count** is used here).

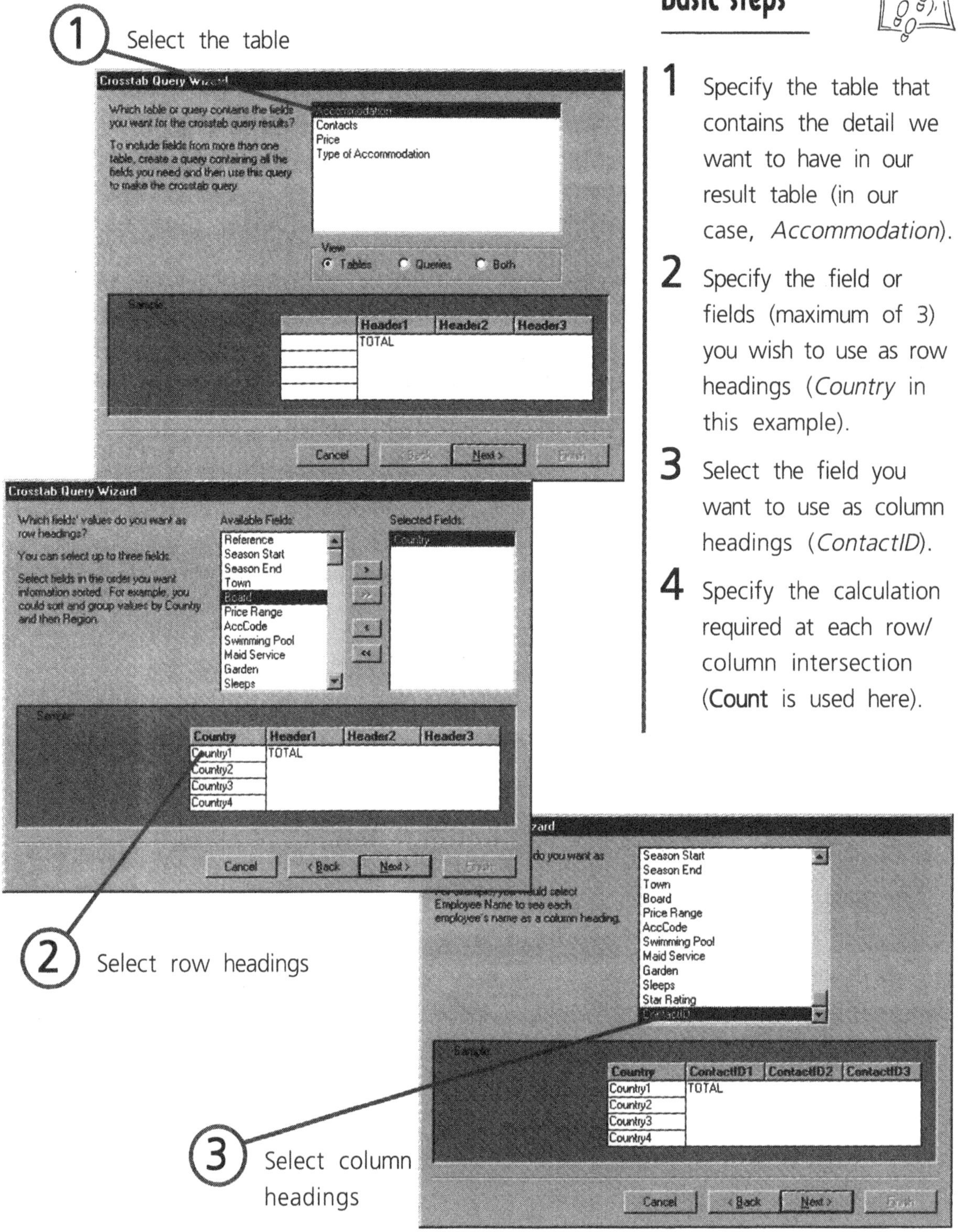

② Select row headings

③ Select column headings

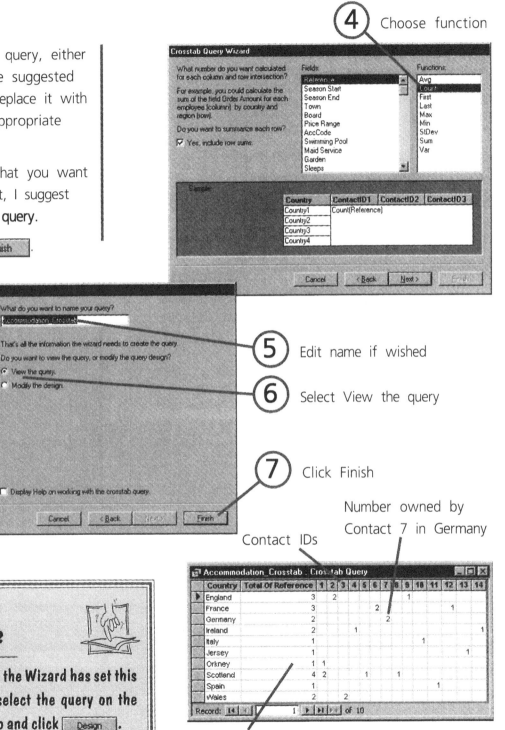

4 Choose function

5 Name the query, either accept the suggested name or replace it with a more appropriate one.

6 Choose what you want to do next, I suggest **View the query.**

7 Click [Finish].

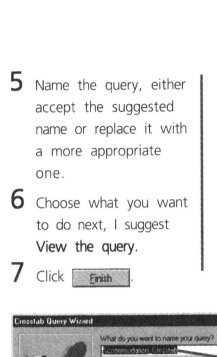

5 Edit name if wished

6 Select View the query

7 Click Finish

Number owned by Contact 7 in Germany

Contact IDs

Take note

To see how the Wizard has set this query up, select the query on the Queries tab and click [Design].

Country	Total Of Reference	1	2	3	4	5	6	7	8	9	10	11	12	13	14
England	3	2								1					
France	3							2				1			
Germany	2							2							
Ireland	2		1												1
Italy	1								1						
Jersey	1												1		
Orkney	1	1													
Scotland	4	2				1			1						
Spain	1										1				
Wales	2		2												

Record: [◄][◄][ ] 1 [►][►►][►*] of 10

Number of properties in each country

109

Summary

❑ If you are trying to **locate specific data** you can use the **Find** command.

❑ To obtain a **subset of the records** in your table you can either Filter By Selection or Filter By Form.

❑ Records can be **sorted** into ascending or descending order.

❑ **Multi-level sorts** must be set up in the Advanced Filter/ Sort dialog box, or as a query.

❑ **Save your query** if you wish to reuse it.

❑ To **interrogate several tables** at the same time, you must set up a query.

❑ **Query criteria** are entered into the Select Query grid.

❑ To **reuse a query**, open it from the Queries tab in the Database window.

❑ To **edit the criteria** in a query that has been saved and closed, select the query on the Queries tab in the Database window and click Design.

❑ You can use a **Query Wizard** to set up a query.

10 Forms

Designing a form

Forms allow you to customise your screen for input and editing purposes, making the screen more 'user friendly'.

We have already used a basic form generated by Autoform in Chapter 6, *Data entry and edit*. In this chapter we will design from scratch a simple tabular form, with data arranged in vertical columns.

The form displays name, telephone number and address details for our contacts.

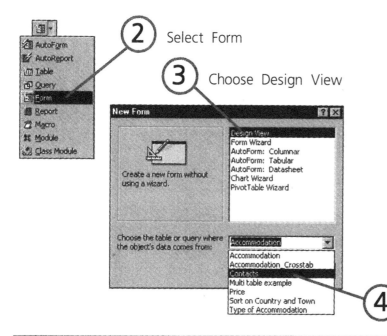

Select Form

Choose Design View

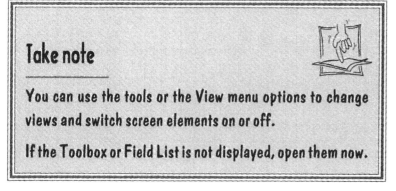

Select the table

1 From the **Forms** tab in the **Database** window, click New .

or

2 Select **Form** from the **New Object** list.

3 At the **New Form** dialog box, select **Design View**.

4 Drop down the list of **tables** and **queries** and choose the table or query (*Contacts* in our case) that supplies data for the form.

5 Click OK .

❑ You arrive at the Form Design screen.

Take note

You can use the tools or the View menu options to change views and switch screen elements on or off.

If the Toolbox or Field List is not displayed, open them now.

The Form Design window

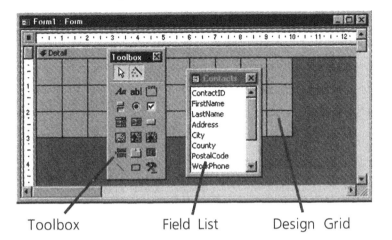

Toolbox   Field List   Design Grid

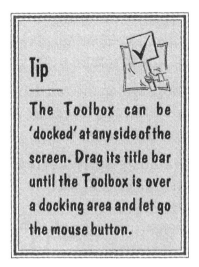

Tip

The Toolbox can be 'docked' at any side of the screen. Drag its title bar until the Toolbox is over a docking area and let go the mouse button.

Take note

We'll use some of these tolls in the next chapter. Check out the others in the on-line Help.

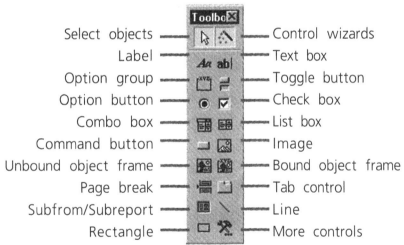

Select objects ———— ———— Control wizards
Label ———— ———— Text box
Option group ———— ———— Toggle button
Option button ———— ———— Check box
Combo box ———— ———— List box
Command button ———— ———— Image
Unbound object frame ———— ———— Bound object frame
Page break ———— ———— Tab control
Subfrom/Subreport ———— ———— Line
Rectangle ———— ———— More controls

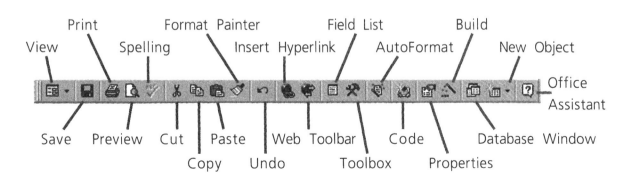

View   Print   Spelling   Format Painter   Insert Hyperlink   Field List   AutoFormat   Build   New Object   Office Assistant

Save   Preview   Cut   Copy   Paste   Undo   Web Toolbar   Toolbox   Code   Properties   Database Window

113

Headers and footers

Usually, you will have some descriptive text in your form. This may be a heading for the whole form, column headings, or simply some narrative with instructions to the user.

In this example we want the form title and some descriptive text. This text, which we will put in the Form Header area, is called a **label**.

We must display the **Form Header** and **Footer** areas first, then insert the labels.

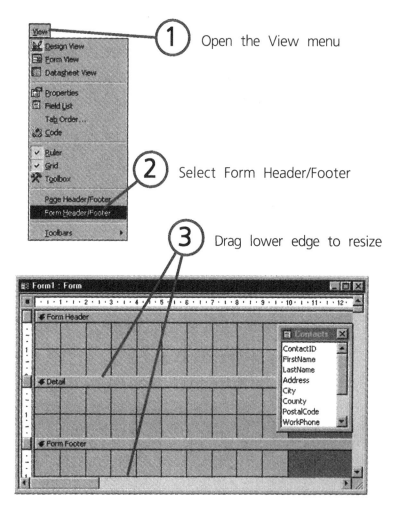

Open the View menu

Select Form Header/Footer

Drag lower edge to resize

Basic steps

1 Open the **View** menu.

2 Choose **Form Header/ Footer**.

❑ A Form Header area appears above, and a Form Footer area appears below, the Detail area.

3 Resize the Form Header and Form Footer area as necessary by dragging the lower edge of the area, up or down (we need to increase the size of the Form Header and decrease the size of the Form Footer – in fact make it disappear!)

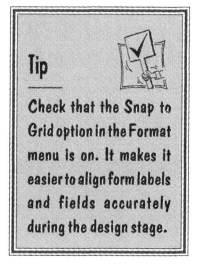

Tip

Check that the Snap to Grid option in the Format menu is on. It makes it easier to align form labels and fields accurately during the design stage.

114

Basic steps

1 Click the **Label** tool [Aa].

2 Move the mouse pointer – now **⁺A** – to where you want your first label.

3 Click and drag to draw a rectangle.

4 Type in your label text e.g. *Property Contacts.*

5 Repeat steps 1-4 for the next label e.g. *Details of Property owners or contacts.*

Adding labels

The headings we are going to put on our form are purely descriptive – they are not part of the table the form is designed around. We can therefore make the text anything we want. This can be very useful for instructions.

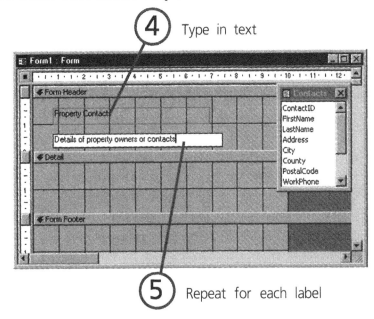

④ Type in text

⑤ Repeat for each label

Adjusting design elements

If you position a label (or any element) incorrectly, or make it too big or small, you can easily fix it. First select it by clicking anywhere on it. Note the handles that appear around the edges of the selected element.

❏ **To Resize**

1 Point to a handle. The pointer changes to a double-headed arrow.

2 Drag the arrow to resize.

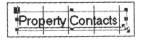

❏ **To Move**

1 Point to an edge (not a handle). The pointer changes to a hand.

2 Drag the element into position.

❏ **To Delete**

1 Press the **[Delete]** key.

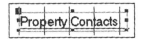

Formatting the labels

Now that your labels are on your form, in the correct position and are the correct size, you might want to enhance the appearance of them so they stand out clearly on your form. You might want to make them bigger, or bolder, or in italics – you choose!

1 Select the label you want to format.

2 To change the font, drop down the list of fonts on the toolbar, and select from there.

3 To change the size of font, choose from the drop-down size list.

4 To make the font **bold**, or in *italics*, click the bold and/or italics tools to switch the option on or off.

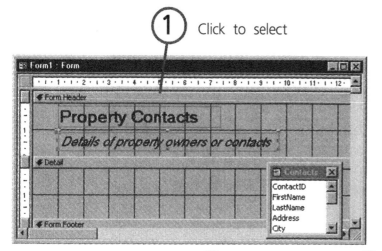

① Click to select

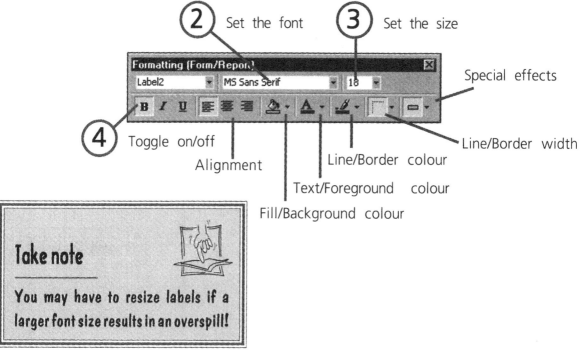

② Set the font   ③ Set the size

Special effects

④ Toggle on/off

Alignment

Line/Border width

Line/Border colour

Text/Foreground colour

Fill/Background colour

Take note

You may have to resize labels if a larger font size results in an overspill!

116

Basic steps

1 Click the Field List tool
🔲 to display the **Field List** (if it isn't visible).

2 Drag a field from the list (*FirstName*), and drop it in the Detail area.

❑ Both components of the field are selected, but we want to deal with them separately.

3 Click on the **field name** section to select it, and press **[Delete]**.

4 If necessary, reposition and/or resize the **field detail** component.

5 Repeat steps 2-4 for each field (*LastName, HomePhone, WorkPhone, Address,* etc) you require.

6 Resize the detail area if necessary.

See page 119 for the final layout.

Adding fields

We now need to position the fields we require in the Detail area of the form. Clicking and dragging the required field from the field list to its destination on the form does this. When a field is dragged over however, it has two components – one for the field name and one for the field detail.

You can leave both parts on your form – or you could delete the field name part (as in this example) and use a label to describe the data.

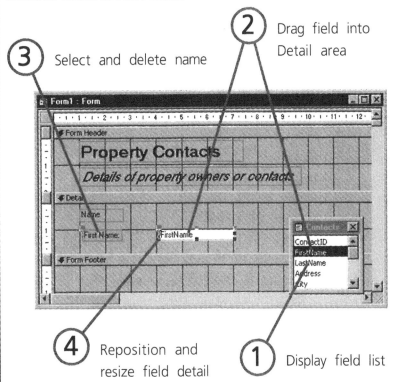

③ Select and delete name

② Drag field into Detail area

④ Reposition and resize field detail

① Display field list

Save your form

Obviously, you need to save your form design if you want to keep it. You can save at any time – you don't need to wait until you have set the whole thing up. If you are designing a complex form, save it regularly.

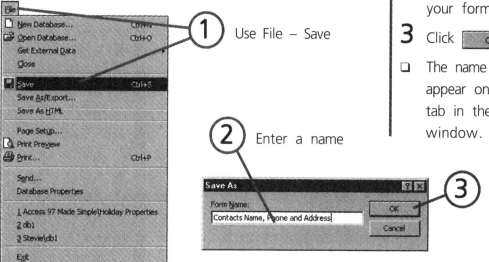

Use File – Save

② Enter a name

③ Click OK

1 Use **File – Save** or click the Save tool 📇.

2 At the **Save As** dialog box, key in a name for your form.

3 Click OK .

❏ The name will be appear on the Forms tab in the Database window.

Save and Save As/Export

If you have already saved your form, and have edited the design since you last saved it, you can use **File – Save** to replace the old version of the form with the new one.

If you want to save the edited version as a separate form, use **File – Save As/Export...** to give a different name. This can be very useful if you are designing several similar forms – once the first is saved, you can edit it as necessary to produce the next, then save it with a different name.

You can copy the form to another database...

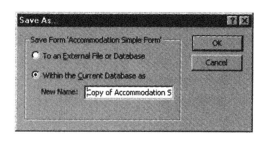

...or copy to the current database

Form View

Basic steps

1 Click the **View** tool 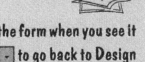 or drop-down the list and choose **Form View**.

❑ The Form is displayed in Form View.

2 Use **[Tab]** to move from field to field.

3 Move from record to record using the forward and backward buttons.

4 Click the New Record button if you wish to add another record.

5 Close your form when you are finished.

Let us look at our form in Form view, where one record will be displayed at a time on the screen.

It is assumed you are in the Form Design screen.

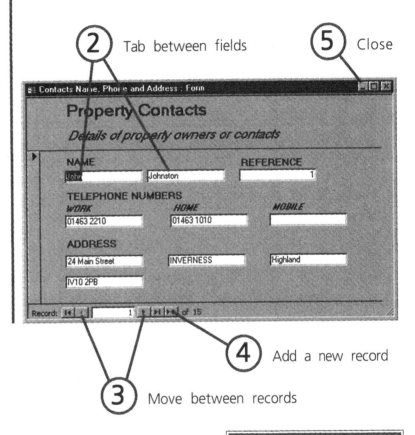

② Tab between fields

⑤ Close

④ Add a new record

③ Move between records

Take note

If you are not happy with the look of the form when you see it in Form View, click the View tool ▨ ▾ to go back to Design View and edit it (remember to save any changes you make).

Take note

Data entered or edited on a form updates the table on which the form is based.

Summary

- **Forms** allow you to customise your input and viewing screens.

- **Headers and Footers** can be used for headings, narrative or instructions you wish to display on your form.

- Your can **add fields** anywhere on your form – simply drag the field required from the field list onto the form grid.

- **Text** (for instructions and/or labels) can be included on your form to enhance its appearance and make it easier to use.

- Forms can be designed from scratch using **Design view**.

- If you **save your form**, it will be listed on the Forms tab in the Database window.

- **Data entered or edited on a form** is fed back to the associated table or query.

11 Reports

The Report Wizard

Reports provide the most effective way of creating a printed copy of data extracted or calculated from the tables and queries in your database. They might be invoices, purchase orders, presentation materials or mailing labels.

Many of the features used in forms design are also used in report design. There are also a number of features that are unique to the report environment. You can build reports from scratch in much the same way as the form we created in the previous chapter – or you could try out some of the Report Wizards.

The example below uses a wizard to create a report that groups our properties by *Star Rating*, and lists details of the *Country*, *Town* and *Type of Accommodation* of each.

Basic steps

1 Click ▐ New ▌ on the **Reports** tab in the Database window or select **Report** from the New Object list.

2 At the **New Report** dialog box, select Report Wizard.

3 Choose the table on which you wish to base your report – *Accommodation* in our case.

4 Click ▐ OK ▌.

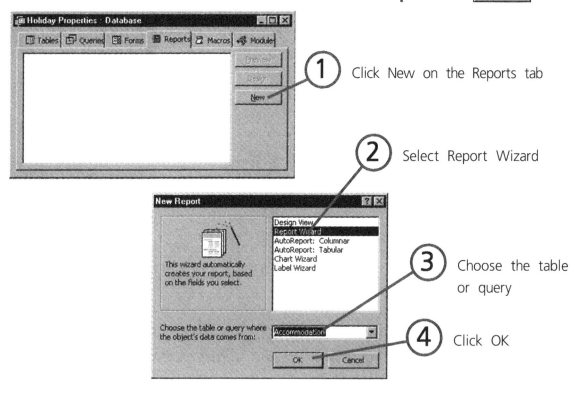

① Click New on the Reports tab

② Select Report Wizard

③ Choose the table or query

④ Click OK

Basic steps

1 Select the fields required for your report.

❏ You can select fields from more than one table if you wish.

2 Specify the *Star Rating* field as the grouping option.

❏ We want all our properties with Star Rating 1 together, all properties with Star Rating 2 together, etc.

cont...

Specifying the detail

The first stages of the Wizard are concerned with the details to be drawn from your database. The later ones specify the appearance of the report.

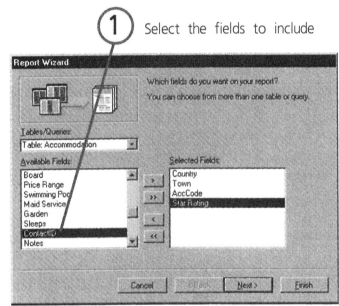

① Select the fields to include

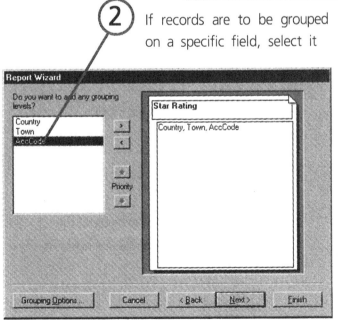

② If records are to be grouped on a specific field, select it

Tip

You can have several levels of grouping, e.g. group first by *Star Rating*, then by *Country*.

③ Do you want to sort your records?

Sort direction

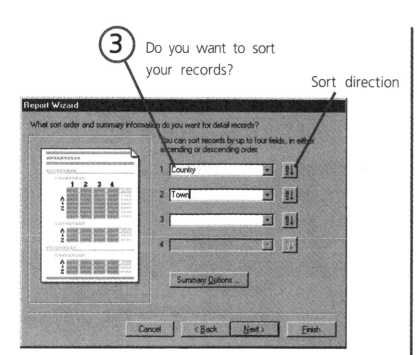

3 Set the sort options required.

4 Choose your report layout options.

5 Select the style you think most appropriate.

6 At the chequered flag, edit the name of your report if you wish.

7 Select Preview the Report.

8 Click [Finish].

④ Specify the layout options

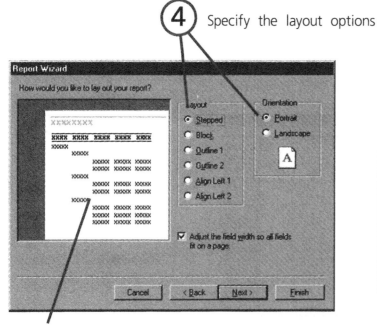

Take note

Remember to click [Next>] when you have completed each step and [Finish] at the chequered flag.

Use the samples to help you decide on the options

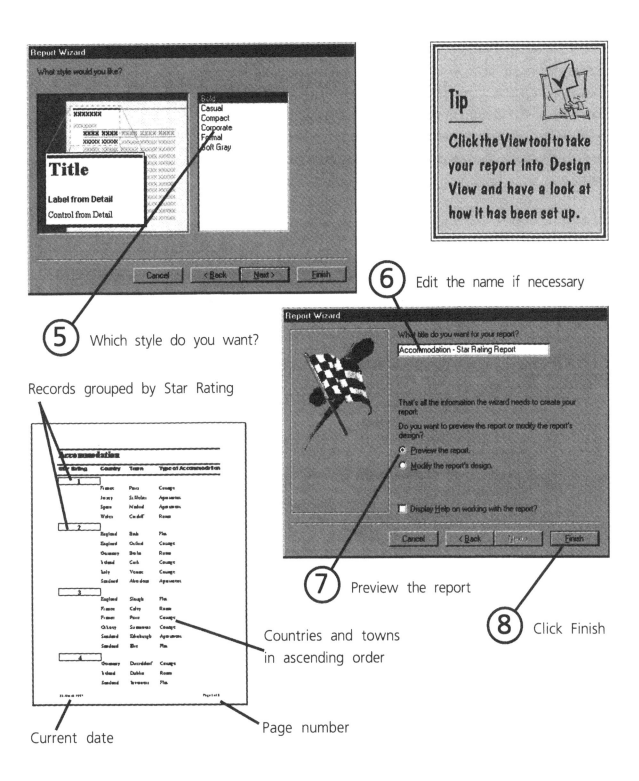

Report Wizard

What style would you like?

Title

Label from Detail

Control from Detail

Bold
Casual
Compact
Corporate
Formal
Soft Gray

Cancel   < Back   Next >   Finish

Tip

Click the View tool to take your report into Design View and have a look at how it has been set up.

(6) Edit the name if necessary

(5) Which style do you want?

Records grouped by Star Rating

Report Wizard

What title do you want for your report?

Accommodation - Star Rating Report

That's all the information the wizard needs to create your report.

Do you want to preview the report or modify the report's design?

◉ Preview the report.
○ Modify the report's design.

☐ Display Help on working with the report?

Cancel   < Back   Next >   Finish

(7) Preview the report

(8) Click Finish

Countries and towns in ascending order

Page number

Current date

125

The design

The design is in essence very similar to what you did when setting up your form, with one or two extra bits that are useful on reports. You can easily change the formatting of any part of the design if you wish – its font size, colour, bold, italics, etc – just select the label, field or text box and use the formatting tools as you did in the form design window.

Labels in Report and Page Header

Group Header

Current date code in Text box

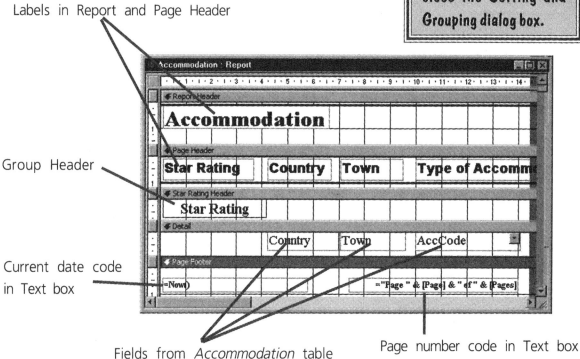

Fields from *Accommodation* table

Page number code in Text box

- The Report Header and Page Header text are Labels that have been formatted.

- The Report Header and Page Header areas can be switched on and off through the View menu.

126

- The *Star Rating* Header is a Group Header. Click the Sorting and Grouping tool to see how this has been set up.

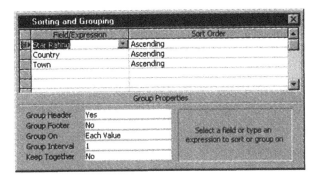

- The Detail area contains fields from the *Accommodation* table.

- The Page Footer contains codes that return the current date *=Now()* and the page numbering format *= "Page " & [Page] "of " & [Pages]* for the report. The codes are entered into Text Boxes, created using the Text Box tool .

- Drawing tools have been used to draw lines and borders around areas of the report. Click the line or rectangle drawing tool, then click and drag on your report to draw the shape. To change the colour or width of the line or border, select it then use the Line/Border colour tool, or Line/Border width tool to get the effect you want.

 Line tool

Rectangle tool

 Line/Border Colour

Line/Border Width

Preview and print

You can Print Preview your report, and print out a hard copy if you wish. There are two Preview choices here. The **Layout Preview** will give you a quick preview using some of your data. The **Print Preview** takes longer to produce, but gives you a preview of all of the data that will appear in your report.

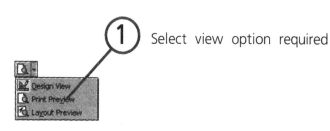

① Select view option required

Basic steps

1 In the Report Design window, click the **Print Preview** tool , or select a preview option from the **View** drop-down list.

2 If the preview looks okay, click the **Print** tool to print your report.

3 Close the **Print Preview** window.

Take note

You can print directly from the Print Design screen, without first doing a preview. Click the Print tool on the Report Design toolbar.

Tip

If you've made changes to the report design, don't forget to save if you want to keep the changes. Click to save.

Take note

If you close the Preview window using the ☐ Close tool on the toolbar, you are returned to the Report Design screen. If you close the Preview window by single-clicking the Close button ☒, you are returned to the Database window.

Mailing labels

Basic steps

1 Click **New** on the Reports tab on the **Database** window or choose **Report** from the **New Object** list.

2 Select **Label Wizard**.

3 Choose the table on which you wish to base your mailing labels – *Contacts* in our case.

4 Click **OK**.

This time, we will create a report to print mailing labels. Again, there is a Wizard, to take us through the steps required to set the labels up.

The mailing labels are for the owners of each property in our database. The name and address details required for the labels are in our *Contacts* table.

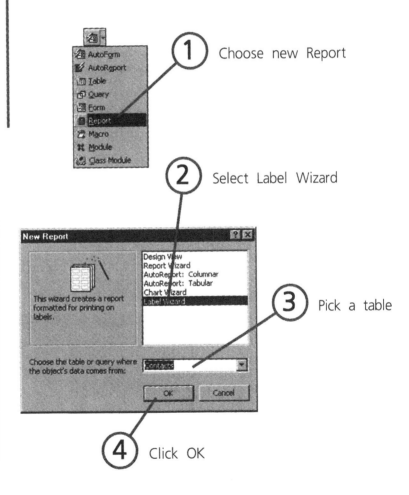

① Choose new Report

② Select Label Wizard

③ Pick a table

④ Click OK

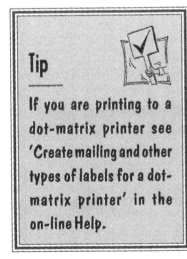

Tip

If you are printing to a dot-matrix printer see 'Create mailing and other types of labels for a dot-matrix printer' in the on-line Help.

Specifying the label design

The next stage is to specify the layout. Getting data to fit comfortably on labels can be a tricky business, so check how they will look – and edit the design if necessary – before you print.

1 Choose the appropriate **label size**, and the **label type**.

2 Change the **Unit of Measure** to suit your labels if necessary.

3 Modify the font style, size, attributes and colour as required.

(1) What size are your labels?

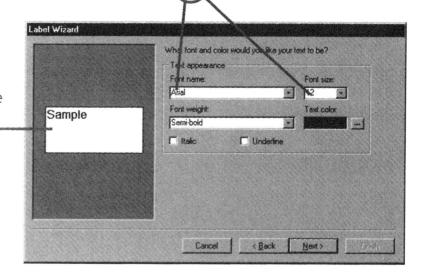

Separate sheets or continuous?

(2) Change as necessary

(3) Set your formatting options

Click Customize to set up non-standard labels

Use the sample to estimate how well your label data will fit using the selected font and size

130

4 Build up the label using the fields found in *Contacts*. Key in spaces, punctuation and text you wish to appear on each label through the keyboard.

5 If you want your labels printed in any specific order, specify the field to sort on.

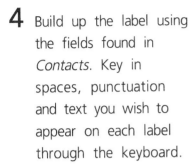

④ Lay out your label

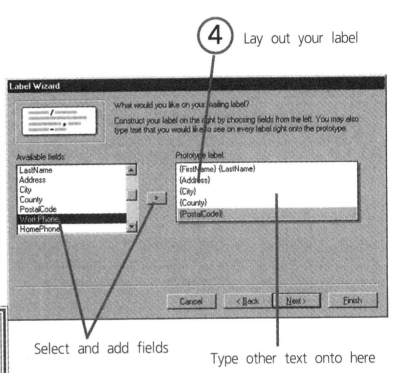

Select and add fields

Type other text onto here

Take note

Remember to click Next> after each step.

⑤ Do you want the labels sorted?

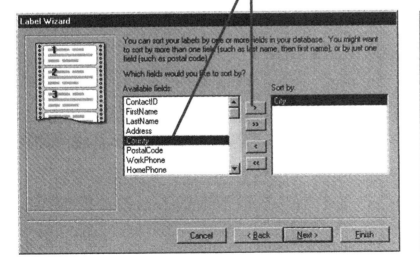

Tip

If you are doing large mailing regularly, talk to the Post Office about their Mail Sort program, with discounts for ready-sorted mail.

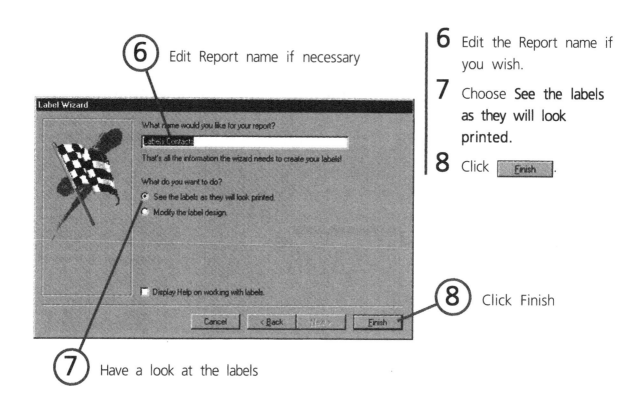

6 Edit Report name if necessary

6 Edit the Report name if you wish.

7 Choose **See the labels as they will look printed.**

8 Click [Finish].

8 Click Finish

7 Have a look at the labels

Print Preview of labels

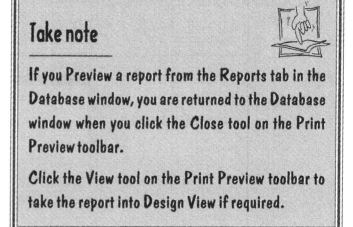

Take note

If you Preview a report from the Reports tab in the Database window, you are returned to the Database window when you click the Close tool on the Print Preview toolbar.

Click the View tool on the Print Preview toolbar to take the report into Design View if required.

Basic steps

1 Check the Preview.

2 Click [Close] to leave the Print Preview and return to the Mailing Labels Design window.

3 Modify the design as required.

4 Click the **Save** tool [🖫] to save the design.

5 **Preview** [🔍] or **Print** [🖨] the labels as required.

6 Close the Report.

❑ You are returned to the Reports tab in the Database window. Your new report should be listed.

Editing the design

The labels are displayed in Print Preview. You can use Page Setup to modify the margins and orientation if necessary, or click the Print tool to print your labels out.

If you want to modify the design of your labels, you must return to Design View by clicking the Close icon on the Print Preview toolbar.

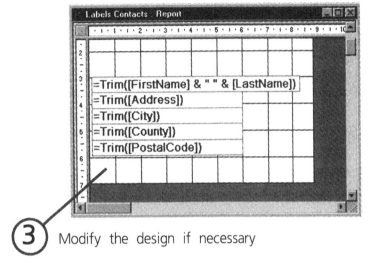

③ Modify the design if necessary

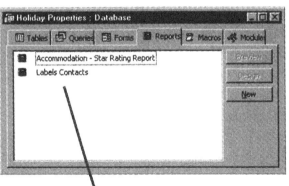

The new report is listed

Take note

The =Trim code removes trailing or leading spaces. This is very useful for address labels, where you want the fields on one line neatly closed up together and not spread out.

The Wizard adds this code to all lines in the address label.

133

Summary

- ❑ **Reports** provide an effective way of presenting data extracted or calculated from your queries and tables.

- ❑ Many of the **techniques used in Form design** are also used in Report design, e.g. placing fields, adding descriptive text, formatting.

- ❑ **Wizards** can speed up the Report design stage.

- ❑ The designs generated by a Wizard can be **customised** to suit your exact requirements.

- ❑ The data in your report can be **sorted and grouped** as required.

- ❑ Codes to display the **current date** or a **page number** can be entered into text boxes

- ❑ The **Drawing tools** can be used to add emphasis to your reports.

- ❑ It is a good idea to **preview your report** before you print – you can then check the layout of your report before you commit it to paper.

- ❑ The Label Wizard simplifies the production of **Mailing Labels**.

12 Database Wizard

Selecting a Wizard

In addition to creating a database from scratch, as we have done in this book, you could use a Database Wizard to help you set up your tables, forms and reports.

There are several ready-made databases that you can modify easily using a Wizard. Have a look through them to see if any could be useful to you.

1 Click the **New Database** tool .

2 Select the **Databases** tab.

3 Pick a database.

4 Click [OK].

5 Create and name your database as shown in Section 3.

(2) Select Databases

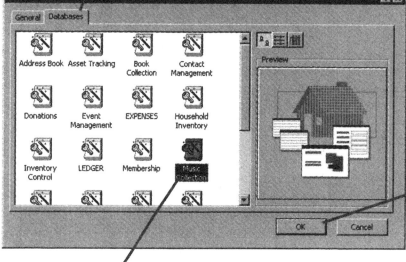

(4) Click OK

(3) Pick a database

Take note

The databases have full sets of fields and predesigned forms and reports. The Wizard simply helps you modify them.

Adding fields

Basic steps

1 Click `Next>` at the introductory panel.

2 Choose a table.

3 Select or deselect the fields as required.

4 Repeat steps 2 and 3 for all the tables.

5 Click `Next>`.

The first thing you need to do is customise the tables in your database. You do this by specifying the fields you want to include or leave out of each table.

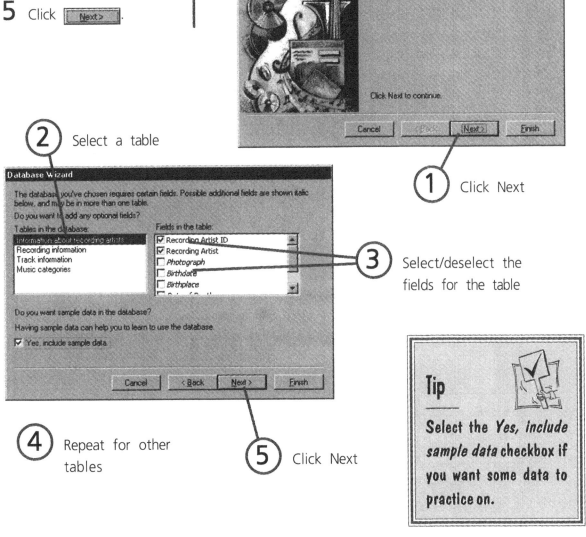

Select a table

Click Next

Select/deselect the fields for the table

Repeat for other tables

Click Next

Tip

Select the *Yes, include sample data* checkbox if you want some data to practice on.

Setting the style

The next steps in the Wizard let you select options that control the screen display and the printed reports. There are several options to choose from – browse through them until you find something you like.

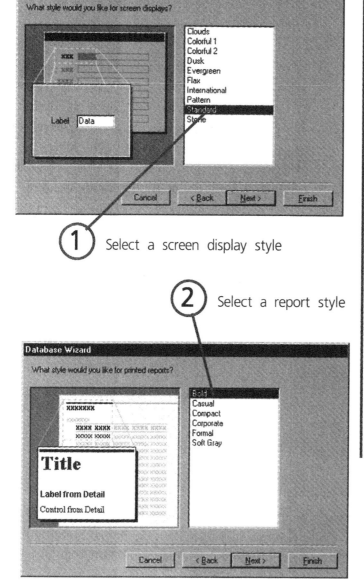

① Select a screen display style

② Select a report style

1 Select a style for the screen display and click `Next>`.

2 At the next step, choose a style for your printed reports in the same way.

3 Give your database a title.

4 Select the **Yes, I'd like to include a picture** box if you want a picture on each report.

5 Click `Picture...` and select the picture from your disk.

6 If you want to start work on the database straight away, select **Yes, start the database** at the final step.

7 Click `Finish` then wait while the Wizard completes your database.

138

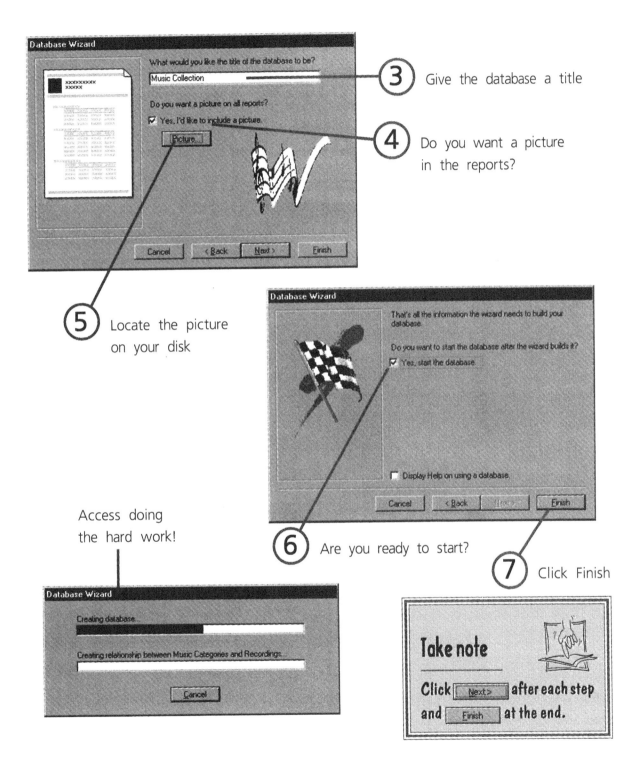

Database Wizard

What would you like the title of the database to be?

Music Collection

③ Give the database a title

Do you want a picture on all reports?

☑ Yes, I'd like to include a picture.

④ Do you want a picture in the reports?

Picture...

Cancel   < Back   Next >   Finish

⑤ Locate the picture on your disk

Database Wizard

That's all the information the wizard needs to build your database.

Do you want to start the database after the wizard builds it?

☑ Yes, start the database.

☐ Display Help on using a database.

Cancel   < Back   Next >   Finish

⑥ Are you ready to start?

Access doing the hard work!

⑦ Click Finish

Database Wizard

Creating database...

Creating relationship between Music Categories and Recordings...

Cancel

Take note

Click [Next >] after each step and [Finish] at the end.

139

The end product

The Switchboard

This acts as a 'front end' to your database, giving easy access to your forms and reports. Some options on the Main Switchboard – Enter/View Other Information and Preview Reports – lead to other Switchboards.

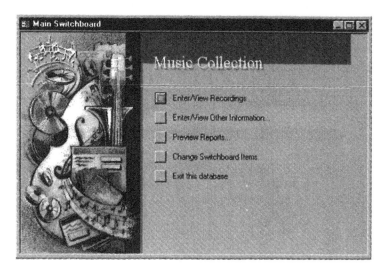

The Main Switchboard of the Music Collection database

Report designs

The Wizard's reports are crisp and clear. If you have chosen to include a picture – perhaps your firm's logo – then that will be incorporated into the design.

The report seen in Print Preview

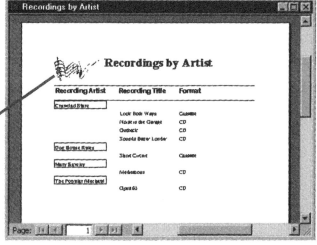

Picture included

Form designs

The standard layouts are well organised and easy to use, but don't forget that you can modify them if you like. Simply take the form into the Form Design window and adjust or enhance it as required.

One of the forms set up by the WIzard for the Music Collection database

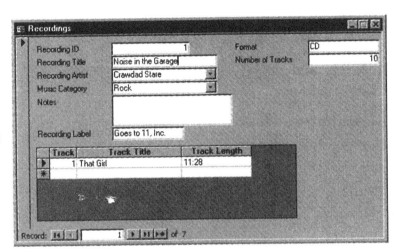

Take note

If the wizards produce tables, forms and reports that suit your needs then they can save you a lot of time by doing the ground work for you.

Summary

- There are several **Database Wizards** for you to choose from.

- You can **customise your tables** by selecting or deselecting the fields for each table.

- There are several **screen display** and **report options** to choose from to set the style for your database.

- **Sample data** can be provided to let you practise using your database.

- **Switchboards** provide a user friendly 'front end' to your forms and reports.

Appendix

Type of Accommodation

AccCode	Description
1	Apartment
2	Cottage
3	Flat
4	Room

Price

Price Range	Jan-Feb	Mar-Apr	May-Jun	Jul-Aug	Sep-Oct	Nov-Dec
A	£240	£260	£300	£350	£310	£260
B	£260	£280	£320	£380	£320	£280
C	£275	£296	£340	£310	£360	£300
D	£285	£310	£370	£420	£390	£350
E	£300	£340	£410	£470	£425	£395

Accommodation

Ref	Season Start	Season End	Type of Accomm	Town	Country	Board	Swim Pool	Maid Serv.	Garden	Price Range	Sleeps	Star Rating	Contact ID
1			A	Aberdeen	Scotland	HB	No	No	Yes	B	4	2	1
2			F	Slough	England	SC	No	Yes	No	C	4	3	2
3	01/02/95	01/12/95	R	Cardiff	Wales	BB	No	Yes	No	B	2	1	3
4			C	Cork	Ireland	SC	No	Yes	Yes	B	4	2	4
5	18/01/95	10/12/95	F	Inverness	Scotland	SC	Yes	Yes	No	D	6	4	5
6			C	Paris	France	SC	No	Yes	Yes	A	4	3	6
7			R	Berlin	Germany	HB	No	Yes	Yes	A	2	2	7
8			C	Dusseldorf	Germany	SC	No	Yes	Yes	B	4	4	7
9			C	Paris	France	SC	No	Yes	Yes	C	6	1	6
10			A	Edinburgh	Scotland	HB	Yes	Yes	No	D	4	3	8
11			F	Bath	England	SC	Yes	Yes	No	D	4	2	9
12			A	Cardiff	Wales	BB	Yes	No	Yes	E	4	4	3
13			F	Elie	Scotland	SC	No	Yes	No	E	4	3	1
14			C	Venice	Italy	SC	Yes	Yes	Yes	C	6	2	10
15			A	Madrid	Spain	SC	Yes	Yes	No	D	4	1	11
16			C	Oxford	England	SC	No	Yes	Yes	C	4	2	2
17			R	Calais	France	BB	No	Yes	Yes	C	2	3	12
18			C	Stromness	Orkney	SC	No	Yes	Yes	B	4	3	1
19			A	St. Helier	Jersey	SC	Yes	Yes	Yes	C	4	1	13
20			R	Dublin	Ireland	HB	Yes	Yes	Yes	D	2	4	14

ContactID	FirstName	LastName	Address	City	County	Post Code	Country	Work Phone	Home Phone
1	John	Johnston	24 Main Street	INVERNESS	Highland	IV10 2PB	Scotland	01463 2210	01463 1010
2	Elaine	Anderson	22 St Stephen Street	EDINBURGH	Midlothian	EH10 3PR	Scotland	0131 442 1021	0131 556 0212
3	Elizabeth	Watson	14 Mill Wynd West	GLASGOW	Strathclyde	G13 3AB	Scotland	0141 665 1043	0141 510 5103
4	Gordon	McPherson	14 Worthington Way	BIRMINGHAM	Midlands	B24 2DS	England	0121 557 9321	0121 676 1999
5	Hanz	Beckenbaur	24 Lang Strasse	BERLIN			Germany	00 49 30 121	00 49 30 435
6	Andrew	Simpson	10 Dolphin Road	LONDON		N18 2WS	England	0181 475 1010	0171 442 4102
7	Alice	Aberley	St Stephens Manse	PETERLEE	Co Durham	SR8 5AJ	England	0191 575 3928	0191 653 1843
8	Brian	Allanson	328 Bath Road	ILFORD	Essex	IG2 6PN	England	0181 543 6758	0171 544 1234
9	Pamela	Johnston	10 Wilson Way	DEREFORD	Norfolk	NR19 1JG	England	01362 331112	01362 574098
10	Joan	Robertson	24 West Linton Way	KENDAL	Cumbria	LA9 6EH	England	01539 561732	01539 665577
11	William	Flux	132 London Road	CARNO	Montgomery	SY17 5LU	Wales	01686 203956	01686 105619
12	Amanda	Wilson	14 High Way	LAMPETER	Dyfed	SA4 8NW	Wales	01570 30651	01570 61234
13	William	Robertson	Hill View Rise	STROMNESS	Orkney	OK10 3AB	Scotland	01856 103212	01856 114322
14	Suzanne	Young	24 Causeway St	CLEMENT	Jersey	J21 2ED	Channel Is	01534 14261	01534 66310
15	Paul	Mitchell	45 Hill Top View	ABERDEEN	Aberdeenshire	AB24	Scotland	01224 10231	01224 54123

Index